Applied Cryptography in .NET and Azure Key Vault

A Practical Guide to Encryption in .NET and .NET Core

COMPUTERS

Stephen Haunts

Foreword by Troy Hunt

Apress®

Applied Cryptography in .NET and Azure Key Vault

Stephen Haunts
Belper, Derbyshire, UK

ISBN-13 (pbk): 978-1-4842-4374-9   ISBN-13 (electronic): 978-1-4842-4375-6
https://doi.org/10.1007/978-1-4842-4375-6

Library of Congress Control Number: 2019932807

Managing Director, Apress Media LLC: Welmoed Spahr
Acquisitions Editor: Joan Murray
Development Editor: Laura Berendson
Coordinating Editor: Nancy Chen

Cover designed by eStudioCalamar

Cover image designed by Freepik (www.freepik.com)

Distributed to the book trade worldwide by Springer Science+Business Media New York, 233 Spring Street, 6th Floor, New York, NY 10013. Phone 1-800-SPRINGER, fax (201) 348-4505, e-mail orders-ny@springer-sbm.com, or visit www.springeronline.com. Apress Media, LLC is a California LLC and the sole member (owner) is Springer Science + Business Media Finance Inc (SSBM Finance Inc). SSBM Finance Inc is a **Delaware** corporation.

For information on translations, please e-mail rights@apress.com, or visit http://www.apress.com/rights-permissions.

Apress titles may be purchased in bulk for academic, corporate, or promotional use. eBook versions and licenses are also available for most titles. For more information, reference our Print and eBook Bulk Sales web page at http://www.apress.com/bulk-sales.

Any source code or other supplementary material referenced by the author in this book is available to readers on GitHub via the book's product page, located at www.apress.com/9781484243749. For more detailed information, please visit http://www.apress.com/source-code.

Printed on acid-free paper

I would like to dedicate this book to my wife, Amanda, and my two kids, Amy and Daniel. Their support makes completing large projects like this much easier when I am sitting on my own in a room trying to write.

Table of Contents

About the Author xi

About the Technical Reviewer xiii

Foreword xv

Introduction xvii

Chapter 1: What Are Data Breaches? 1

Types of Data in a Breach and Their Consequences 2

The Impact on a Company 4

    Financial Loss 4

    Legal Action 4

    Regulatory Impact 5

    Loss of Reputation 5

Why Network Protection Isn't Enough 6

How Can Developers Help? 6

    What Can You Expect from This Book? 7

What You Will Learn 7

    .NET Standard and .NET Core 9

Code Samples in This Book 10

Chapter 2: A Brief History of Cryptography 11

Ancient Times 11

Increasing Cipher Complexity 13

    Enigma and Mechanical Ciphers 15

Modern Cryptography 18

    Symmetric Encryption 18

    Public and Private Key Cryptography 19

Why Is Cryptography Important?...20

    Examples of Modern Cryptography 21

The Four Pillars of Modern Cryptography 22

    Confidentiality..22

    Integrity 22

    Authentication 22

    Non-Repudiation..23

Summary..23

Chapter 3: The Importance of Random Numbers.................................25

Generating Deterministic Random Numbers...26

Generating Secure Random Numbers 27

Summary..30

Chapter 4: Hashing and Hashed Message Authentication Codes 31

Hashing and Integrity..31

MD5..33

Secure Hash Algorithm (SHA) Family 35

Authenticated Hashing..39

Summary..45

Chapter 5: Safely Storing Passwords 47

Storing Passwords in the Clear..47

Encrypting Passwords 48

Using Hashes to Store Passwords 49

Using Password Based Key Derivation Functions 54

Summary..60

Chapter 6: Symmetric Encryption...61

Symmetric Encryption..61

    Advantage: Very Secure...62

    Advantage: Fast...62

    Disadvantage: Sharing Keys Is Hard..62

    Disadvantage: Dangerous If Compromised..63

History of DES and Triple DES 63

How DES and Triple DES Works.. 65

History of AES 67

How AES Works 68

    How Secure Is AES Against Brute-Force Attacks?... 69

    API Commonality in the .NET Framework 70

    AesManaged and AesCryptoServiceProvider 73

Performing Symmetric Encryption with .NET.. 74

Summary.. 84

Chapter 7: Asymmetric Encryption.. 85

Advantage: Very Secure 85

Advantage: Fast 86

Disadvantage: Sharing Keys Is Hard 86

Disadvantage: Dangerous If Compromised 86

What Is Asymmetric Encryption? 87

The History of RSA 88

How Does RSA Work? 88

    Key Derivation 88

    Encryption and Decryption 90

RSA in .NET 91

    In-Memory Keys 91

    XML-Based Keys.. 92

    Cryptographic Service Provider.. 93

    Encryption and Decryption 95

Summary.. 100

Chapter 8: Digital Signatures.. 101

High-Level Look at Digital Signatures.. 102

Digital Signatures in .NET 106

Summary.. 112

Chapter 9: Hybrid Encryption 113

Combining Symmetric and Asymmetric 115

Adding Integrity Checks 126

Securely Comparing Byte Arrays 132

Extending with Digital Signatures 134

Summary 141

Chapter 10: Key Storage and Azure Key Vault 143

Exploring Key Management Options 143

Introducing Azure Key Vault 145

Azure Key Vault Hardware Mode 146

Azure Key Vault Software Mode 146

Keys vs. Secrets 146

Azure Key Vault Example Costs 147

Setting up Azure Key Vault 148

Creating a Key Vault 149

Registering Your Application with Azure Active Directory 150

Authorize Your Application to Use Keys and Secrets 153

Manually Creating Keys and Secrets 155

Azure Key Vault "Hello World" Application 158

Summary 168

Chapter 11: Azure Key Vault Usage Patterns 169

Multiple Environments 169

Configuration as Secrets 173

Local Key Wrapping 175

Exploring Key Wrapping Further 182

Key Rotation and Versioning 183

Password Protection 184

Varying the Iterations over Time 191

Digital Signing 192

Upgrading the Hybrid Encryption Example 195

Summary.. 205

Chapter 12: Final Summary 207

Cryptography Summary 208

Random Numbers.. 208

Hashing and Authentication.. 209

Storing Passwords.. 210

Symmetric Encryption 211

Asymmetric Encryption 213

Digital Signatures 214

Hybrid Encryption 215

Azure Key Vault... 217

Don't Forget the Perimeter... 219

Next Steps... 220

Index.. 223

About the Author

 **Stephen Haunts** has been a software developer for the last 25 years, working in many industries, such as video games, financial services, insurance, and healthcare. One of his main specialties is security and cryptography, and he has implemented a range of techniques into many systems at many companies, including financial lenders, insurance claims management companies, and global banks. Stephen regularly speaks at conferences and user groups about secure coding in .NET, and he has authored a highly rated cryptography course for Pluralsight.

About the Technical Reviewer

Eric Potter is a software architect for Aptera Software and a Microsoft MVP for Visual Studio and Development Technologies. He works primarily in the .NET web platform, but loves opportunities to try out other stacks. He has been developing high-quality custom software solutions since 2001. At Aptera, he has successfully delivered solutions for clients in a wide variety of industries. He loves to dabble in new and exciting technologies. In his spare time, he loves to tinker with Arduino projects. He fondly remembers what it was like to develop software for the Palm OS. He has an amazing wife and five wonderful children. He blogs at `http://humbletoolsmith.com`, and you can follow him on Twitter as @pottereric.

Foreword

Assume breach. That's pretty much the point we've reached in the industry now where we need to resign ourselves to the fact that despite our best efforts, the likelihood of an attacker gaining access to our systems is alarmingly high. I started Have I Been Pwned in 2013 with 154 million breached records from a small handful of incidents. Fast forward only a few years, and its many billions of records across hundreds of individual data breaches. And that's just scratching the surface of what lies beneath; there are an untold number of incidents that we, the public, will never know about. In many cases, the service owners themselves don't even know, or it takes years to discover the extent of or even the *existence* of a data breach. I'm not talking about small fly-by-night services here either; I'm talking about some of the web's largest services, such as Dropbox, LinkedIn, and MySpace.

It's fascinating to look at how these incidents occur because the root causes span such a diverse set of exploits. Software vulnerabilities remain prevalent (SQL injection is still considered the number one application security risk today[1]), databases are regularly left publicly facing without a password and insiders are both deliberately and inadvertently exposing data. In one recent case, we even learned that one of our local Aussie banks may have lost customer records off the back of a truck—not metaphorically either, *literally*. Maybe the auditors called in to investigate the breach reported that "Forensic investigators hired to assess the breach retraced the route of the truck to determine whether they could locate the drives along this route but were unable to find any trace of them."[2]

This is why cryptography matters. It matters because it's an essential part of the answer when organisations ask how they can better protect themselves from the types of incidents described above. It matters because we're increasingly realising that data protection goes well beyond the controls that keep adversaries from accessing the data in the first place and extend all the way to protecting the data itself.

---

[1]https://www.owasp.org/index.php/Top_10-2017_A1-Injection
[2]https://www.buzzfeed.com/paulfarrell/australias-largest-bank-lost-the-personal-financial

Like Stephen, I've spent the last two and a half decades building software in all sorts of capacities, most recently in my role as a Microsoft Regional Director (an honorary title). During that time, I've seen some huge changes in the industry but without doubt, the most significant has been the move to cloud computing. Microsoft has played a significant role in that shift with their Azure platform and it's changed so many of the ways we deliver applications; the way we code, the way we scale and yes, even the way we encrypt. Key Vault has brought secure and accessible cryptographic storage to the masses and addressed a fundamental problem we've been tackling for years: how to correctly store secrets in our software.

I've known Stephen for many years now and have always enjoyed seeing him talk about cryptography. It's one of those niche subjects within application security which is a niche itself within the software development discipline. I've often joked that I know enough about cryptography to know how much I don't know, which probably also explains why I always take something away from Stephen's talks.

We've never had more cryptography than we have today. More than three quarters of all web traffic is encrypted,[3] our families and friends are socialising on networks with end-to-end encryption like WhatsApp and iMessage and we're walking around with supercomputers in our pockets which encrypt all data at rest. Encryption has come to the masses and just as it's now more accessible than ever to the general public, it's also more accessible than ever for those us of building software. Stephen's approach to applied cryptography on Microsoft's platform will help you continue that trend by introducing more cryptography into your own development. I hope you enjoy hearing from him as much as I have over the years and that maybe, just maybe, this book even takes some work off my plate and prevents a few data breaches!

—Troy Hunt
Founder of *Have I Been Pwned*

---

[3]https://letsencrypt.org/stats/

Introduction

I like the choice of words that Troy Hunt used in the foreword for this book, "assume breach." Those two words sum up the entire existence of this book and why I wrote it. Organizations today need to adopt this mindset change and realize that they will most likely suffer a data breach at some point in their existence. Sure, you may have spent a fortune on firewalls and intrusion detection systems, and indeed these are good investments, but what about the disgruntled operations engineer who was recently passed up for promotion or a pay rise and decides he wants payback? I am not trying to pick on operations staff deliberately, but I mean anyone inside the organization who has some level of production access to data or developers who routinely use cuts of production data in their test environments; please stop doing this...

How do you stop that data from being taken outside the organization? Of course, you might be using at-rest encryption for your databases, and that is great, but what if this malicious insider does a "select *" query over a series of tables, pastes the results into a spreadsheet, and makes a copy of the file. At-rest encryption isn't going to help you then. This data could contain sensitive personal information that relates to individuals, and it is this personal information that gives the data value because it can then be used to mount social engineering and impersonation attacks against your customers.

Instead of just relying on encryption at rest, we need to add an extra layer of encryption at the database row-level and ensure the keys used to encrypt this data are appropriately managed, and that is where this book comes in. If you are like me, then you are a software developer working in a team producing software for your organization. You are most likely not a dedicated security professional but a general software developer. These are the types of people that this book for. Time and time again in my career, I have seen security features pushed back in a schedule for more visible features that are perceived to add more value to the company; but although security features are less visible, they are just as important, if not more important, than the domain system features.

As a developer, I can emphasize with you when this happens, and this book is my way of helping you. When I started designing this book, there were different approaches I could have taken. I could have written a 700-page reference manual in which I documented every class, method, and property used for security in .NET, but if you are like me, then you probably wouldn't read it. Instead, my goal was to make this book as short as possible, yet packed with information, which is why this book takes you through the cryptography primitives available in .NET/.NET Core and shows you how to use them to build something secure with key management in Azure Key Vault. I want you to be able to work through the book fairly quickly and have the provided source code be useful to you, so that you can easily adopt it in your systems.

It isn't my goal to turn you into a master cryptographer; it is my goal to arm you with enough tools and sample code so that you can incorporate better security without it being seen as a "burden" on your business sponsors. Even a small bit of encryption with well-managed keys is better than nothing at all. As we have already stated, you should assume a data breach is going to happen, but if that breached data has encrypted personal information and encrypted sensitive data with properly manages keys, then that data becomes near worthless.

A breach notification system, like Have I Been Pwned, is designed to notify people when a data breach has occurred, but if a person's personal data (including email address) is encrypted, then the data is more anonymous and can't be tied back to a physical person. The last thing you want as an organization is to appear as a breach in Have I Been Pwned with unencrypted personal details, payment card data, and passwords. Breaches that appear in Troy's system end up becoming public, and Troy appears on news channels around the world to discuss the breaches that give a company a bad reputation. The impact of a data breach can be drastically lessened when important data is encrypted.

So, on that note, I hope that you enjoy this book, and I wish you every success in making your systems more secure. Cryptography is actually good fun when you get your head around the subject.

CHAPTER 1

What Are Data Breaches?

We live in a technical society that is both exciting and terrifying at the same time. Never before have we had instant access to information and services at the touch of a button—from the devices we carry in our pockets, the computers on our desks, or the TVs in our houses. While this unprecedented level of access to online services is exciting, it also brings a lot of personal risks. To access these services, we have to give up our information to companies that we must entrust with it. Unfortunately, although we trust these companies with our data, we are continually hearing in the news about data accounts being stolen.

First, let's discuss what a data breach means. A data breach is where the sensitive or confidential data that a company is responsible for holding has been viewed by, used by, or stolen by a person who is unauthorized to do so. A data breach can happen for a lot of reasons. For example, an employee at a company could deliberately or accidentally copy or reveal information to someone who is not authorized to view it. Another example is someone who has inadvertently left a phone, laptop, or USB memory stick on a train or in a café. While this may be accidental as opposed to a deliberate action, it is still a data breach. Another example, and the one that is reported in the press the most, is when someone outside of an organization manages to infiltrate a company's IT systems and steal data. This could be through hacking and taking advantage of exploits in the system, or by coercing a staff member through social engineering.

Just how prevalent are data breaches? There are some fantastic resources online that illustrate just how much of a problem data breaches are, but I want to draw your attention to one in particular on a website called Have I Been Pwned, by security researcher, speaker, and trainer, Troy Hunt (see Figure 1-1).

© Stephen Haunts 2019
S. Haunts, *Applied Cryptography in .NET and Azure Key Vault*,
https://doi.org/10.1007/978-1-4842-4375-6_1

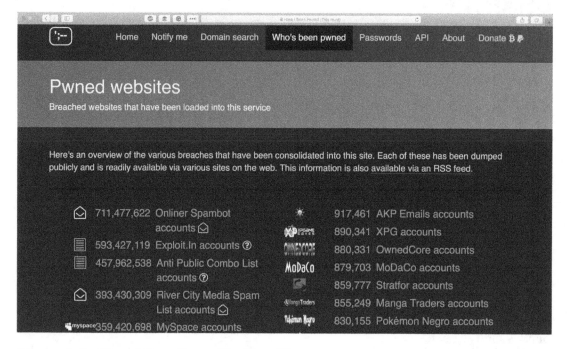

Figure 1-1. *Have I Been Pwned by Troy Hunt*

Have I Been Pwned is a breach notification service that enables you to sign up for notifications when your email address shows up in any data breaches that are made public. I have been a member of this site for many years, and I have been notified many times that my email address was included in data leaked from various companies. I want to mention this website because it also shows startling numbers that illustrate just how big a problem breached data is. As you are reading this, I invite you to go to site at www. haveibeenpwned.com and click the "Who's been pwned" link. This takes you to a page that contains information on companies that have had data breaches and the number of records that have been leaked. What should strike you is the sheer size of some of these numbers for companies such as LinkedIn, with over 160 million records; Adobe, with over 150 million records; and Domino's Pizza, with over 600 thousand records. These are huge numbers, and if you look at the website, the list of companies that have had data stolen goes on and on.

Types of Data in a Breach and Their Consequences

When we talk about breached data, what kinds of data does it include? Typically, it is Personally Identifiable Information (PII), which is data used to identify a living person, such as your name, postal address, phone number, and email address. Breached data could also include sensitive information, such as credit card numbers, and health information, such as prescriptions. This data has a lot of value to people on the black market because it helps with identify theft. When breached data includes unencrypted credit card numbers, it can be used to make online purchases, leaving the owner of that data with a financial loss. These risks are very worrying, and as well as just being inconvenient, the result of some of these data breaches can have a genuine human impact.

A prime example of this was the Ashley Madison data breach in 2015. Ashley Madison is a dating website for people looking to have extramarital affairs. In 2015, a hacking group called the Impact Team stole the site members' personal data. The Impact Group threatened to release the members' personal information if the website was not immediately shut down. Ashley Madison didn't comply with this request, and on August 18, 2015, the group leaked more than 25 GB of the site members' data onto the Internet.

Setting aside the nature of this website, imagine if you were a site member having extramarital affairs. How would you feel? No doubt, very nervous that your partner would find out. Shortly after the leak of this data, many Internet sites appeared to let you publicly search this information for someone's name or email address. This enabled suspicious wives, husbands, or partners to search for information. You can only imagine the fallout from this, as many people's relationships broke down and divorces were filed. Many celebrities and government officials were also exposed, which had an impact on their careers. Not only does being exposed like this affect the people involved directly, but imagine the hurt it can also cause families and children. Sadly, there were even a few suicides reported due to this data breach.

The reason I mention the Ashley Madison data breach is to explicitly highlight the human consequences that a data breach can cause. I am not only talking about stolen money from a credit card, or someone's identity impersonated to apply for credit, although these are very serious in their own right, I am talking about actual consequences to people's lives and families. No matter what your personal opinion is about a website like this, the people that signed up for the service should expect that the company would look after their data and assume that the data would be kept private. In other words, it is the company's responsibility to look after private and personally identifiable information correctly.

Securely looking after personal data is a difficult problem to solve, and it can be an expensive problem for companies to deal with secure storage of data. Unfortunately, there is still an attitude with some companies that they are too small to be attacked, and that criminals go after bigger companies. I have worked for many businesses that have taken this view. Sadly, this just isn't true. In fact, if you are a smaller company, you are more likely to be a target because it could be easier to break into your systems. This is why the information in this book could mean the difference of your data being safe should it be stolen.

The Impact on a Company

I have talked about the victims' consequences when their data is stolen, but what about a company who has been targeted? The effects can come in many forms.

Financial Loss

The first impact is financial loss to the company. Larger organizations may be able to swallow the costs, but this could run into millions of dollars. For smaller companies, this might be much harder to accept. Financial loss could happen for many reasons. The first is that bad press could cause sales loss for a company's products or services. The financial loss includes measures to deal with security improvements after the fact, which is always the wrong time to implement them. Preventative measures are still more cost-effective than post-breach operational measures, which are always more expensive to implement. For smaller organizations, the cost of lost revenue and post-breach security measures could quickly put a company out of business.

Legal Action

Another cost that can severely impact a business is legal action from the victims of the data theft. If victims lodge legal claims against the company, these costs could have a severe financial impact, which could drive a smaller organization into insolvency. Imagine if your business loses customers' credit card information, which are leads the criminals to steal money from your customers. It is entirely possible for the credit card companies or the issuing financial institutions to file claims against your company.

Regulatory Impact

Penalties handed down by regulatory bodies have a direct financial impact on organizations that suffer data breaches. For example, if you lose credit card information, then you may have stiff fines because of violations of PCI-DSS (Payment Card Industry – Data Security Standard) regulations. I have worked for a financial organization that suffered a breach of customer cards, which resulted in hefty fines. These fines are designed to be large enough to cause pain to the companies involved.

The financial services industry isn't the only regulated industry that can hand down penalties. The healthcare industry is monitored to protect patient data. Medical records are very sensitive and private, and if not handled carefully, customers or patients can suffer a lot of distress, so the fines are sized to act as a harsh punishment to the organizations involved.

In addition to industry-specific regulatory bodies monitoring companies, each country has government regulatory bodies to protect the consumer. In the European Union, for example, this comes in the form of regulations, such as the General Data Protection Regulation (GDPR). Any company that trades with an EU company has to comply with these regulations, and the rules governing GDPR and the safe storage of personal information are rigorous.

Loss of Reputation

All the impacts and penalties discussed so far are very serious and can cause a company significant problems if they are experienced in the event of a data breach, but by far the most severe impact a company can face is that of reputational damage. Trust between a company and its customers is very hard to build, yet very easy to lose. If your business encounters a data breach that is then exposed in the press, it is very likely that you will lose the trust of your customers, and they will take their business elsewhere. Overnight, this could drastically impact business revenue streams. Loss of revenue, coupled with stiff financial penalties from regulators, can be tough to recover from. Larger companies can bounce back, but it is a very steep uphill struggle. Smaller organizations might not be so lucky, and the impact can force them out of business.

All of these impacts can be devastating to an organization, but you can protect yourself from the consequences. While it might not be entirely possible to entirely outsmart determined career criminals, if you make your security sturdy enough, attackers will go elsewhere. There are two main ways to build suitable deterrents: a robust network security and robust software security.

Why Network Protection Isn't Enough

The first method that companies adopt to protect themselves from a data breach is the investment in networking hardware, such as firewalls and intrusion detection systems. These are very wise purchasing decisions, and any company serious about network security should spend in this area, whether physical hardware placed in own data centers or cloud-based abstractions with providers such as Microsoft Azure or Amazon AWS. These systems help keep criminals out and build a toughened perimeter around the network.

It is also common to have systems running within a network that monitors traffic going over the network to detect personal information being sent into or out of the company. I personally fell afoul of such a system when I worked for a large Internet bank in the United Kingdom. I was working on a system for handling payments from debit cards for loan accounts. As part of our testing of the system, I emailed example debit card numbers and example loan account numbers to a testing colleague. These were not real numbers, only test data, but the day after sending these to my colleague, I was taken aside by my manager and asked to explain the data. In this case, it was just test data, and it was sent to an internal staff member, so there were no repercussions, but these same systems would detect real data being sent outside the company by any operational staff. All of these methods are vital to the security of businesses, but these systems are not enough on their own, and more can be done by the people building the enterprise systems used by organizations to perform business.

How Can Developers Help?

If you are reading this book, then it is probably safe to assume that you are a software developer. As a developer, there is a lot you can do to help ensure the safety of your employer and its customers. I firmly believe that it is the duty of any software developer to do all they can to protect the data of their company's customers. You can do this by understanding some of the tools available to you.

It doesn't matter what industry you work in—financial services, insurance, healthcare, manufacturing, defense—or even a small software development agency producing software as a service solution, the protection of personal information is essential. Using the techniques and tools presented throughout this book, you will be armed with the knowledge, skills, and behaviors to build robust systems to protect your employer and its customers. You have the power to make a real difference in the fight against data breaches and their far-reaching consequences.

This book focuses specifically on the Microsoft .NET Framework and the newer .NET Core 2+ and .NET Standard 2+ platforms. This means that you have the tools to build cross-platform, secure, back-end solutions installed in an on-premise data center or in the cloud, and hosted on Windows or Linux servers.

What Can You Expect from This Book?

When I started planning this book, there were several different routes to present the information. I could have written a large reference book that talked about every method and property on every security-based class in .NET, but I felt that this would not be useful because that information is available in Microsofts' documentation, and it would have made the book huge. As a developer, I understand the pressure that you face to develop code quickly and on a budget. Your time is precious. I wanted to make this book useful but not take long to read and work through.

Instead of a reference manual, I put together a book that takes you through some of the important cryptographic primitives available in .NET and Azure Key Vault, and shows you how to combine them to create secure applications. This book is very practical in the way that it is presented. I urge you to download the accompanying source code files so that you can experiment with the code. Let's now look at how the book is broken down.

What You Will Learn

In this book, I take you through all the cryptographic primitives available to you in .NET, and then show you how to use them together to create robust encryption, key management, and password storage mechanisms in your software solutions. The chapters are broken down as follows.

In Chapter 2, I walk through a brief history of cryptography, from ancient times to modern techniques. Cryptography has a fascinating history, and by taking a brief look at its roots, you get a good appreciation of the methods in use today. Once we have taken a look at the history, we look at some of the properties of modern cryptography, such as confidentiality, integrity, authentication, and non-repudiation.

One of the foundations of modern cryptography involves the ability to generate random numbers. In Chapter 3, I talk about why this is important and the best way to create numbers using the tools available in .NET. In our exploration of random numbers, we jump into the practical elements of this book.

Once we have looked at how to generate random numbers, we move to the concepts around integrity and authentication by looking at hashing and hashed message authentication codes. I will cover various hashing algorithms, such MD-5, SHA-1, and SHA-256/SHA-512, and use hashed message authentication codes to provide authentication, which provide the necessary building blocks to move to the next chapter.

Safely storing passwords is something that seems so easy on the surface; it's just saving some data in a database. Frequently, this is done incorrectly, and it becomes a significant problem with data breaches because stored passwords are often stolen and easily cracked, giving attackers a way to access and take over accounts on systems. In Chapter 5, we explore some of the conventional techniques for storing passwords and look at why they are no longer good enough for future systems. At the end of that chapter, you will have the knowledge and skills needed to perform password storage correctly using libraries that are included in .NET.

In Chapter 6, we look at how to implement confidentiality in your systems with encryption algorithms, such as DES, Triple DES, and AES. Symmetric encryption encompasses a series of algorithms that use the same key to both encrypt and decrypt data. I also talk about the issues of key sharing with symmetric encryption. Sharing symmetric keys is very hard to do securely, which leads us to the next chapter.

Asymmetric encryption is a form of encryption similar to symmetric encryption, except there is one fundamental difference. Instead of using the same key for encryption and decryption, you use a mathematically linked pair of keys called a public and a private key. This type of algorithm gives unique properties to add to our cryptography toolkit. In Chapter 7, we focus on the RSA encryption algorithm.

Following on our look at asymmetric encryption, in Chapter 8, we look at another use for RSA for generating digital signatures. This helps us fulfill our non-repudiation property, which means we can help a sender prove that they sent a message, so there is no denying it in the future.

By Chapter 9, we will have covered all the main cryptographic primitives that we need to satisfy confidentiality, integrity, authentication, and non-repudiation. In this chapter, we combine these primitives to create a hybrid encryption protocol, where we use all the benefits of each primitive to develop robust encryption protocols to use in your enterprise systems. By the end of this chapter, we will have built up a working set of code libraries that you can use in your systems.

Once we have looked at symmetric and asymmetric encryption, in Chapter 10 look at ways of storing these encryption keys. One very robust way of doing this is with hardware security modules, which are hardware appliances designed to go into a data center to securely store encryption keys. We focus on a particular implementation called the Azure Key Vault, which is a very cost-effective and secure way to store keys.

Once you are familiar with the Azure Key Vault, in Chapter 11, we look at patterns and practices for its use in the real world. This includes both operational and software development patterns. Using the techniques discussed in this chapter, you will be able to significantly lower the cost of using Key Vault.

In the final chapter, I summarize all the key points of the book, and then look at how data encryption fits with other system technologies and best practices to help you in the future. Not all data breaches start with technology. They can start with social engineering attacks against staff, so a combination of good technical and personnel practices can help a company survive in the digital age.

.NET Standard and .NET Core

All the code has been written to conform with .NET Standard 2.0, which means the code works with both .NET Core 2 and higher and .NET Framework 4 and higher. Before .NET Standard 2.0, which was released in the summer of 2017, many of the cryptography techniques discussed in this book were not supported in .NET Core (version 1.1), which means everything presented in this book would only work on the original .NET Framework and could only be run on Windows operating systems.

.NET Standard 2 and .NET Core 2 are now both available, and in full use, so everything in this book works across Windows, Linux, and macOS operating systems. This is excellent news for developers because it offers a lot of choice in how we write and deploy our code. In fact, all the code samples in this book were developed using Visual Studio for Mac, and then tested in Visual Studio for Windows.

Code Samples in This Book

All of the code discussed in this book is available from GitHub `https://github.com/Apress/applied-crypto-.net-azure`. The solution file can be opened on Visual Studio for Mac or Windows. You can also use the JetBrains Rider IDE to work with the code samples. As you progress through this book, I recommend you download the source code and experiment with the examples. All the code in the samples fully work and can be used in your applications to enable the full power of cryptography.

Let's now move on to the next chapter, where we look at a brief history of cryptography, and I introduce some of the leading features of cryptography.

CHAPTER 2

A Brief History of Cryptography

The art of cryptography has been around since the human race first communicated in written form. In its earliest form, cryptography, or encryption, involved taking written notes and applying a mathematical process to it to make the message unreadable. Then the recipient could use the same method, known only to them and the sender, to recover the message.

When using cryptography, the original text that you want to encrypt is referred to as *plaintext*. It is called plaintext because, in its original form, it is just text. Once plaintext has been encrypted, it is referred to as *ciphertext*. The terms plaintext and ciphertext have been around almost as long as cryptography itself, and they are still used today, even though we are not encrypting text on paper, but as bits and bytes on a computer.

Like most technical innovations, cryptography was developed to be a communications method in times of war. Most great innovations came out of armed conflict, and cryptography is no exception.

Ancient Times

If we take a look at the ancient Greeks, they favored a technique for encrypting messages by wrapping paper around a wooden pole of a particular diameter. They wrote the message on the paper while it was wrapped around the pole, and then unwound it and transported the message to its recipient. The recipient would then wrap the paper around another pole of the same diameter, which revealed the message. If the poles were not the same diameter, then the message would not be readable.

© Stephen Haunts 2019
S. Haunts, *Applied Cryptography in .NET and Azure Key Vault*,
https://doi.org/10.1007/978-1-4842-4375-6_2

This may seem very rudimentary by today's standards, but at the time, it was very effective. The key for the message wasn't a passphrase or key, but a wooden pole of a particular diameter.

The Romans popularized an encryption technique called the Caesar cipher. It worked by shifting letters in the alphabet by a certain number of characters, generally three places. This means that in plaintext, A becomes D, B becomes E, C becomes F, and so on. So, the message "meet me at dawn" becomes "phhw ph dw gdzq" when the alphabet is shifted by three characters. To decrypt the message back to "meet me at dawn," you just perform the reverse operation by shifting three places in the opposite direction.

Both the stick cipher and the Caesar cipher are known as a *monoalphabetic substitution cipher*, which means there is only one alphabet used for encryption and decryption. Ancient Greeks encrypted and decrypted a message with a pole of a fixed diameter. Romans used a single alphabet. The common key between encrypting and decrypting a message was the number of letters to shift by, three in the example we worked through.

As you can imagine, both of these techniques are very easy to break. With the stick cipher, you can try different diameter poles until you can read the message, and with the Caesar cipher, you try different shift positions until you can understand the message. Although the techniques were effective during their time, it didn't take long before the ciphers were broken by anyone intercepting the messages.

Another way in which a monoalphabetic cipher can be broken is by performing frequency analysis of the ciphertext. Frequency analysis involves counting the number of times each letter appears in a message. Then by using knowledge and the rules of the English language, you can make certain assumptions—such as vowels like "a" and "e" are the most frequent letters used. Using this knowledge, letters with a high frequency rate can be substituted with the common vowels until you start to see word patterns forming. The longer the ciphertext, the easier this frequency analysis and pattern matching becomes.

The ease of breaking monoalphabetic ciphers meant that new encryption methods needed to be invented. This gave rise to the *polyalphabetic cipher*. With a monoalphabetic cipher, only one alphabet is used. With a polyalphabetic cipher, multiple alphabets are used. This works by frequently switching alphabets during the encryption process. The reason you do this is to make frequency analysis harder to achieve because the same letter in plaintext might appear as several different letters in ciphertext, which has the effect of flattening out the histogram created when performing frequency analysis. This makes finding patterns in words much harder.

Increasing Cipher Complexity

The first known polyalphabetic cipher is believed to be the Alberti cipher by Leo Battista Alberti from around 1467. This cipher used multiple alphabets to encrypt a message. Alberti switched alphabets many times during the encryption of a message. He indicated that the alphabet should be changed by including an uppercase letter or a number in the plaintext.

In 1470, Alberti developed a cipher disc to make encrypting and decrypting easier. This disc consisted of two circular plates, one larger than the other. The small plate was mounted on the larger plate and could rotate freely. These early cipher discs were made of copper and had the alphabet, in the correct alphabetic order, inscribed on the circumference of the outer plate. The inner plate had an alphabet written on it, but this alphabet was mixed. The outer plate was called the *stationary*, and the inner plate was called the *moveable*.

When encrypting a message, the inner disc was turned to a starting position so that the outer disc's letter A was opposite the inner disc's letter F. This was the starting position. Encrypting the message began when the person found the plaintext letter on the outer disc and wrote down the corresponding letter from the inner rotor. Not moving the inner rotor during the message encryption would create a standard monoalphabetic cipher, but the disc was designed to rotate throughout the encryption of the message, which made it a polyalphabetic cipher. Turning the disc one position for every letter of plaintext encrypted created a very effective encryption scheme that made frequency analysis very hard to achieve.

Another variation of the Alberti cipher is the Vigenère cipher devised by Blaise de Vigenère. At the time, this cipher was believed to be unbreakable and earned the nickname *le chiffre indéchiffrable*. The Vigenère cipher is a polyalphabetic cipher that uses a series of intertwined Caesar ciphers based on the letters of a key word. The cipher worked by using a grid with the alphabet written along the top and the side of the square. The alphabet was written on each line but shifted by one character (see Figure 2-1).

	A	B	C	D	E	F	G	H	I	J	K	L	M	N	O	P	Q	R	S	T	U	V	W	X	Y	Z
A	A	B	C	D	E	F	G	H	I	J	K	L	M	N	O	P	Q	R	S	T	U	V	W	X	Y	Z
B	B	C	D	E	F	G	H	I	J	K	L	M	N	O	P	Q	R	S	T	U	V	W	X	Y	Z	A
C	C	D	E	F	G	H	I	J	K	L	M	N	O	P	Q	R	S	T	U	V	W	X	Y	Z	A	B
D	D	E	F	G	H	I	J	K	L	M	N	O	P	Q	R	S	T	U	V	W	X	Y	Z	A	B	C
E	E	F	G	H	I	J	K	L	M	N	O	P	Q	R	S	T	U	V	W	X	Y	Z	A	B	C	D
F	F	G	H	I	J	K	L	M	N	O	P	Q	R	S	T	U	V	W	X	Y	Z	A	B	C	D	E
G	G	H	I	J	K	L	M	N	O	P	Q	R	S	T	U	V	W	X	Y	Z	A	B	C	D	E	F
H	H	I	J	K	L	M	N	O	P	Q	R	S	T	U	V	W	X	Y	Z	A	B	C	D	E	F	G
I	I	J	K	L	M	N	O	P	Q	R	S	T	U	V	W	X	Y	Z	A	B	C	D	E	F	G	H
J	J	K	L	M	N	O	P	Q	R	S	T	U	V	W	X	Y	Z	A	B	C	D	E	F	G	H	I
K	K	L	M	N	O	P	Q	R	S	T	U	V	W	X	Y	Z	A	B	C	D	E	F	G	H	I	J
L	L	M	N	O	P	Q	R	S	T	U	V	W	X	Y	Z	A	B	C	D	E	F	G	H	I	J	K
M	M	N	O	P	Q	R	S	T	U	V	W	X	Y	Z	A	B	C	D	E	F	G	H	I	J	K	L
N	N	O	P	Q	R	S	T	U	V	W	X	Y	Z	A	B	C	D	E	F	G	H	I	J	K	L	M
O	O	P	Q	R	S	T	U	V	W	X	Y	Z	A	B	C	D	E	F	G	H	I	J	K	L	M	N
P	P	Q	R	S	T	U	V	W	X	Y	Z	A	B	C	D	E	F	G	H	I	J	K	L	M	N	O
Q	Q	R	S	T	U	V	W	X	Y	Z	A	B	C	D	E	F	G	H	I	J	K	L	M	N	O	P
R	R	S	T	U	V	W	X	Y	Z	A	B	C	D	E	F	G	H	I	J	K	L	M	N	O	P	Q
S	S	T	U	V	W	X	Y	Z	A	B	C	D	E	F	G	H	I	J	K	L	M	N	O	P	Q	R
T	T	U	V	W	X	Y	Z	A	B	C	D	E	F	G	H	I	J	K	L	M	N	O	P	Q	R	S
U	U	V	W	X	Y	Z	A	B	C	D	E	F	G	H	I	J	K	L	M	N	O	P	Q	R	S	T
V	V	W	X	Y	Z	A	B	C	D	E	F	G	H	I	J	K	L	M	N	O	P	Q	R	S	T	U
W	W	X	Y	Z	A	B	C	D	E	F	G	H	I	J	K	L	M	N	O	P	Q	R	S	T	U	V
X	X	Y	Z	A	B	C	D	E	F	G	H	I	J	K	L	M	N	O	P	Q	R	S	T	U	V	W
Y	Y	Z	A	B	C	D	E	F	G	H	I	J	K	L	M	N	O	P	Q	R	S	T	U	V	W	Y
Z	Z	A	B	C	D	E	F	G	H	I	J	K	L	M	N	O	P	Q	R	S	T	U	V	W	Y	Z

Figure 2-1. *Vigenère cipher*

A key phrase was chose, which was repeated in the message (see Figure 2-2). For example, if the message was "meet me at noon" and the key phrase was "secret key," you would end up with the following.

plaintext	m	e	e	t	m	e	a	t	n	o	o	n
key stream	s	e	c	r	e	t	k	e	y	s	e	c

Figure 2-2. *Vigenère cipher key stream*

To encrypt the message, you looked for the letter from the key along the top of the grid and then look down that column until you reached the row that contained the letter from the plaintext. In this case, the first key letter is s and the plaintext letter is m. First, we find the s along the top of the grid and look down the column until we reach the row that corresponds with m. This gives us the letter e. If we do this for the entire "meetmeatnoon" plaintext, we end up with "eigkqxkxlgsp" ciphertext. Notice that all spaces from the messages have been removed because spaces in ciphertext could give an attacker a clue about the words in the message. The Vigenère cipher was so secure that it was not broken for nearly three centuries.

The Vigenère cipher was very easy to implement, which meant it was easy to use as a field cipher in times of war if used in conjunction with cipher discs similar to the Alberti cipher. A good example of this occurred during the American Civil War. The Confederates used a brass cipher disc to implement the Vigenère cipher successfully.

The main weakness of the Vigenère cipher is the repeating key phrase that is used during the encryption process. If an attacker can guess the length of the key phrase, it is easier to decipher the message because they are treated like an intertwined series of Caesar ciphers, which can be broken individually. With that said, however, it was considered the gold standard of encryption for hundreds of years.

Enigma and Mechanical Ciphers

The ciphers discussed so far are manual ciphers because they are handled by a person with pen and paper. The twentieth century saw cryptography become machine automated. The most famous example is the Enigma Electronic Rotor machine used during World War II.

There were lots of variations of the Enigma machine, and early versions were cracked by hand at Bletchley Park in the United Kingdom. There was a variant of the Enigma used by the German Naval Fleet (see Figure 2-3), although it was much harder to break. To break the German version of the Enigma, a Bletchley Park team headed up by Alan Turing and Gordon Welchman created a code-cracking machine called the Bombe in August 1940. It helped automate the cracking of ciphertext from the naval Enigma. This machine and work by Alan Turing and his team helped win the battle in the Atlantic, which helped change the course of World War II.

Figure 2-3. *The Enigma machine (Source: Central Intelligence Agency)*

The Enigma machine resembled a typewriter. It featured a series of mechanical rotors, a keyboard, an illuminated series of letters and a plug board that allowed you to insert short cables. The Enigma machine came with a set of five rotors, three of which were used in the machine.

The machine had 26 keys representing each letter of the alphabet. The letters were only uppercase. The keyboard did not contain any numbers, punctuation characters, carriage returns, or a space bar.

The plug board at the front of the machine contained 26 sockets. Each of these sockets had a letter printed next to it. To connect these sockets, ten leads had plugs on each end. If you plugged the leads into two sockets labeled A and Y, it had the effect of swapping the letters around. This meant that if the machine generated the letter A, it was substituted with a Y. The same was also true the other way around. If the machine generated a Y, it was substituted with an A.

Each of the five rotors that came with Enigma was surrounded by a rotating ring that could be fixed into 26 positions, each representing a letter of the alphabet. The rotor locked into the machine with a pin. Out of the five rotors, three could be placed into the machine at any one time. The rotors attached to the machine with a spindle and set to a predetermined position. This predetermined position represented part of the secret settings that set up the machine for encryption.

Once the machine was configured for use, as the operator pressed a key on the keyboard, the rotors turned one step at a time and one rotor at a time. The signal flowed from the keyboard in the plug board, through the rotors, in both directions, and through another lead on the plug board before lighting up one of the lamps, which indicated a letter. The machine operator wrote down this letter to form the encrypted message.

I mentioned that the machine settings form the secret key for encrypting and decrypting a message, but what do these settings look like? The Enigma operator was provided a codebook at midnight on any particular day. The codebook's settings informed the operator how to configure the machine. The codebook gave five sets of settings each day to form the configuration.

The first setting in the codebook was the date on which the setting was valid. Next, was the rotor order, which stated which three of the five rotors had to be loaded into the machine and in what order. Next, the codebook indicated the rotor position for each rotor. Each rotor had to be turned to point to a specific letter setting. Next, the codebook contained the plug board settings, which told the operator which sets of letters to connect with the ten included cables. This parameter might be set to something like AR, WC, SD, GH, UF, XV, BL, PM, ZO, TY, KN. Once the machine was configured, the operator could encrypt three letters, whose results were included at the start of the message. This worked as a check for the recipient to know the machine had been configured correctly.

The contents of these codebooks were highly classified, and the German operators were under strict instruction that if they were ever in a position to be captured or in a situation where the enemy could seize the machines, they had to destroy the machines and codebooks.

Modern Cryptography

Machines like the Enigma and the many variations of rotor machines were the first era in automating cryptography. After World War II, as we entered the digital age, a new breed of cryptography was needed. This new cryptography had to work efficiently with modern computers, which meant working at a bits and bytes level instead of working with standard alphabets. While it is beyond the scope of this book to cover all developments in this space, let's cover a few highlights in the advent of modern cryptography.

Symmetric Encryption

In 1973, a German mathematician named Horst Feistel published an article titled "Cryptography and Computer Privacy" in *Scientific American* magazine. The article discussed a new form of cryptography, which became known as a Feistel network. The Feistel network became the basis for many of the modern cryptographic algorithms in use today. The most popular is the Data Encryption Standard (DES), which was published in 1997 by the National Bureau of Standards (NBS) in a joint venture with IBM, where Horst Feistel worked.

Although the DES standard was set by NBS and IBM, the National Security Agency (NSA) insisted on modifications to the algorithm. The most prominent was changing the key size from 128 bits to 56 bits. NSA enforced modifications to give them a better chance at breaking the algorithm using special computer equipment. The reduction in key size eventually undid DES. Since the key length was reduced to 56 bits, and the Feistel network worked on 64-bit blocks, eight additional parity bits needed to be added to the input data because it is split to feed onto the blocks.

We look at DES as part of the .NET Framework later in this book. The internals of these algorithms are complicated, but the good news is that you don't need to understand the inner workings to use them.

The DES algorithm is called a *symmetric encryption algorithm*, which means that the same key used to encrypt data is the same key that is used to decrypt the data. This is similar, in principle, to polyalphabetic ciphers.

In 1997, a competition called the DES Challenge (DESCHALL) ended after 140 days of trying to break a DES algorithm through a massive distributed computing effort on the Internet. It was done by a brute-force attack, trying different key combinations out of a total key space of 72 quadrillion keys. The attack worked by having a single server controlling the keys. This server acted as the brain for the entire operation.

Each computer that took part in the challenge had to ask for a range of keys from the key server and then report their result. The key server also logged the unique IP addresses of the machines involved and reported that over 78,000 individual machines took part in the challenge.

Even though DES was cracked and compromised, a variation of DES called Triple DES, or 3DES, uses three iterations of DES to encrypt data. I talk about Triple DES in more detail later in the book.

DES was starting to show its age, and a three-year long public contest was launched in 1997 by the National Institute of Standards and Technology (NIST) to find a new encryption standard. In 1999, five finalists were narrowed down from more than 15 submissions. These finalists were algorithms such as Rijndael, RC6, Twofish, Mars, and Serpent. The submissions had to conform to two main requirements. The block size had to be 128 bits and the algorithm had to be fast and efficient. The winner was the Rijndael cipher, which was developed by two Belgian cryptographers, Joan Daemen and Vincent Rijmen. I talk about the Advanced Encryption Standard (AES) later in the book.

Public and Private Key Cryptography

The modern cryptographic algorithms discussed so far are all examples of a *symmetric algorithm*, which means that you use the same key for both encryption and decryption. Current symmetric algorithms—like DES, Triple DES, and AES—are very efficient at encrypting large amounts of data, but the main drawback of these algorithms is that it is very hard to share the keys between multiple parties. If you were to use the same key to encrypt and decrypt data, you need to make sure your recipient also has the same key. With this in mind, how do you get that key to someone else? Do you email it? That is not a good idea because it could be intercepted in transit. Do you post the key? Again, this could be intercepted. You could physically give the other person the key, but this is impractical. What you need is a viable alternative, which is where public and private key cryptography comes in.

One of the most common algorithms for this, which is explored later in the book, is RSA. RSA was designed in 1977 by Ron Rivest, Adi Shamir, and Len Adleman at MIT. The algorithm's name, RSA, is the initials of each of their surnames.

Whereas ciphers like DES and AES are algorithmic by nature and designed to work with large amounts of data, RSA is mathematical by nature and is based on modular arithmetic. They keys are based on prime numbers, and RSA's security comes from the fact that it is currently impossible to factor a large prime number into its constituent primes. An excellent way to build a mental model of this is that the public key is a huge prime number and the private key contains the numbers that are multiplied together to form the public key.

Anyone can know the public key; hence, the name *public*; the recipient only knows the private key. You encrypt data with the recipient's public key, and the recipient uses their private key to decrypt the message.

There is a limitation to RSA, though, in the amount of data you can encrypt in one go. You cannot encrypt data that is larger than the size of the key, which is typically 1024 bits, 2048 bits, or 4096 bits. You could break down your data into smaller chunks and encrypt it, but this is inefficient. One of the topics that we tackle later in the book is using RSA and AES together to build a hybrid encryption scheme.

If you wish to learn more about the history of cryptography, I can recommend two books. *The Code Book* by Simon Singh (Anchor, 2000) is a fairly short book, but it is a fascinating read. If you want to go into a lot more depth, then I recommend *The Code-Breakers* by David Kahn (The Macmillan Company, 1967). This book goes into a tremendous amount of depth about the history of cryptography.

Why Is Cryptography Important?

Cryptography allows people to have the same confidence they have in the real world in the electronic world. It enables people to do business electronically without worry of wrongdoing by others. Every day, millions of people interact electronically, whether it is through email, ecommerce (on sites like Amazon), or on ATMs or cellular phones. The significant increase of information transmitted over the Internet or on private networks has led to an increased reliance on cryptography.

Cryptography makes the Internet more secure and the safe transmission of electronic data possible. For a website to be protected, all the data transmitted between the computers must be encrypted. This allows people to do online banking and online shopping with their credit cards, without worrying that any of their account information is being compromised. Cryptography is essential to the continued growth of the Internet and electronic commerce.

Examples of Modern Cryptography

We have talked a lot about how cryptography has been used in times of war, but what are some of the uses for modern cryptography? First is online shopping. Whenever you buy something from a website like Amazon, your transaction is done behind SSL, and your payment card information is encrypted. This is a level of protection that everyone has come to expect. Shopping online has become something that people take for granted these days, and it is cryptography that helps to ensure that shopping experiences are done safely.

The next example is authenticating with different systems or websites. To access various systems, you need to prove who you are. This is commonly done by authenticating yourself with a username and password. We cover secure password passing later.

Every time you put your bank card into an ATM and enter your pin, cryptography is used behind the scenes. This includes validating the pin number and authenticating the user. The communication between the ATM and the bank is also encrypted to protect a customer's transaction. Because the bank is issuing cash to a customer, there is a good deal of integrity checking in play, and even non-repudiation, so that once money has been released, the customer cannot deny that cash was given to them.

These days, everyone has a cell phone and wants to make calls that are private. Modern digital cell phones employ cryptography to encrypt the phone call to help make this possible. Modern smartphones are also powerful computers in their own right. They connect to the Internet either via a cellular network or over Wi-Fi. As with a desktop computer, smartphones also use cryptography algorithms like SSL to protect traffic flowing on the Internet.

Another example of cryptography is the rise of the digital currency like Bitcoin. Bitcoin is a peer-to-peer payment processing system and digital currency in which users transact directly without an intermediary. Transactions are verified by network nodes and reported in a public distributed ledger called a *blockchain*. Bitcoin is commonly referred to as a *cryptocurrency*, because cryptography is at the heart of how the currency works.

A final example of cryptography is electronic voting. The concept of election vote verification through cryptography has emerged in academic papers to introduce transparency and trust in electronic voting systems. It will allow voters to verify that their votes have been recorded and counted correctly.

The examples of cryptography shown in this chapter are just a few in the real world. The one thing that you can be sure of is that cryptography and encryption are everywhere, so it is essential for developers to understand some of the cryptography tools available to them in their platform of choice.

The Four Pillars of Modern Cryptography

In modern cryptography, there are four core problems or pillars to solve: confidentiality, integrity, authentication, and non-repudiation.

Confidentiality

Confidentiality is commonly associated with cryptography and encryption. It is where you take data and encrypt it to be in a form that cannot be read by someone else. There are lots of different cryptographic algorithms in use today, and in this book, we look at DES, Triple DES, AES, and RSA.

Integrity

Data integrity is about maintaining and proving accuracy and consistency in the data sent between two parties. This means that if someone sends data to a third party, that individual should be able to detect if the data has been corrupted or tampered with in any way. I cover some different cryptography primitives that you can use to help enforce data integrity, including hashing algorithms such as MD5, and Secure Hash Algorithms, such as SHA-1, SHA-256, and SHA-512.

Authentication

Authentication is about establishing the identity of a person or system sending a message. A good example is with SSL certificates on a web server proving the identity of the server that you wish to connect to. The identity is authenticated by use of a cryptographic key. A less secure key means that there is lower trust between two parties. Authentication is also commonly used by everyone when they enter their username and password to gain access to a system. Your Facebook or Twitter account is an excellent example of this. To use those systems, you have to authenticate yourself with the Facebook or the Twitter website to prove who you are. We look at authentication when we discuss hash message authentication codes (HMACs) later in the book.

Non-Repudiation

Non-repudiation is about proving that someone has carried out an action or signed a document. A signature on a paper contract is a good example of this. If a contract has been signed and witnessed, then that person cannot deny having signed the agreement. This metaphor also carries into the digital world. In this book, I cover digital signatures that use the RSA cryptographic primitive.

Summary

In this chapter, we explored the history of cryptography through the ages. Ever since humans could communicate in writing, there has been a desire to communicate in code so that enemies cannot read intercepted messages. In the earliest days, encryption was based on simple alphabets, and then substitution ciphers, but in the digital age, complex symmetric and asymmetric encryption algorithms are available.

In this modern age, throughout your day you use encryption and cryptography—when you use your phone or your secure Internet connection, or buy goods on the Internet. Cryptography is fundamentally important to the very fabric of our lives as we rely on it to keep our data safe and secure.

CHAPTER 3

The Importance of Random Numbers

The encryption algorithms discussed in Chapter 2 require a source of random data to generate new symmetric keys. Most computers do not have a hardware-based random number generator, so software developers need to use a software-based implementation to generate random numbers that are suitable.

Because random numbers are generated in software, they are rarely completely random; they are typically *pseudorandom*; that is, they appear random, but are not random. To create random data, you need a source of entropy or random input.

Modern cryptographic algorithms are built around Kerckhoff's principle, which states that the "security of the system must depend solely on the key material, and not on the design of the system." This means that the strength of modern cryptographic algorithms is determined by the number of bits an attacker needs to guess to break the algorithm. In this book, for example, we use 256-bit keys (32 bytes) with AES and 2048- and 4096-bit keys with RSA. The strength also implies that a potential attacker does not know of any of the bits used in the encryption keys. The strength of a key and algorithm starts to diminish when new attacks against the algorithm are found, and any of the keys can be derived by looking at the encrypted output.

Some random-number generators ask you to move your mouse or use your keyboard as a source of that entropy; others take events such as hard-drive activity or network activity for their source of entropy. Entropy is a measure of uncertainty or randomness associated with data. Creating entropy through physical movements typically works well for computer workstations but can be a problem in some cases, such as server hardware with a network card, some Flash RAM, and CPUs. A network appliance that performs encryption has no good sources of entropy, apart from network events, which an attacker could manipulate to their advantage. Before we look at implementation of a reliable random number generator, let's take a look at the common `System.Random` class that is in .NET.

© Stephen Haunts 2019
S. Haunts, *Applied Cryptography in .NET and Azure Key Vault*,
https://doi.org/10.1007/978-1-4842-4375-6_3

25

Generating Deterministic Random Numbers

Before becoming familiar with cryptography in .NET, you might have used the random number generator in the System namespace. This is fine for simple scenarios like creating lottery numbers or simulating a dice roll, because it gives the appearance of randomness if you provide a different seed value every time. If you provide the same initial seed value, you will get the same numbers out of the random number generator when you run it. This deterministic nature is no good for generating secure cryptographic random numbers.

To use the System.Random number generator, you must first create an instance of the class and provide a seed value. This seed value is a starting value to initialize the random number generator.

```
using System;

public class Example
{
    public static void Main()
    {
        Random rnd = new Random(1234);

        for (int ctr = 0; ctr < 10; ctr++) {
            Console.Write("{0,3}   ", rnd.Next(-10, 11));
        }
    }
}
```

If you provide the same seed value into different random-number generator instances, then you will generate the same set of random numbers. If creating a deterministic series of numbers is what you require, then this way of using System. Random is perfectly fine. You may need to generate deterministic test data or example for your unit tests. If you wanted to ensure that you create different random numbers each time, then you should make your seed value time-dependent, which means that you are guaranteed a different seed value every time.

While using a time-variant seed value offers more random and non-deterministic numbers, it is not recommended for generating random numbers suitable for cryptography. Another issue with System.Random is that it is not thread safe; so if you are using `System.Random`, you need to use thread locking around each call. Let's not dwell on `System.Random` any longer, and instead look at a better solution, which is `RNGCryptoServiceProvider`.

Generating Secure Random Numbers

As you have seen, random numbers are critical in using cryptography efficiently because we need good, non-deterministic random numbers to create symmetric and asymmetric encryption keys.

`System.Random` is not very good at generating non-deterministic random numbers. To produce cryptographically secure random numbers, the `RNGCryptoServiceProvider` class uses an internal Windows cryptographic service provider to create the number. `RNGCryptoServiceProvider` is a much safer way of generating these numbers, and it is the technique that Microsoft recommends. The trade-off for securer random numbers is that `RNGCryptoServiceProvider` is much slower to execute compared to `System.Random`, but this is a small trade-off when you want to deal with numbers being generated to use as encryption keys.

`RNGCryptoServiceProvider` internally uses an implementation called `CryptGenRandom` and more specifically a function called `RtlGenRandom` to generate its random numbers. This random number function uses entropy from the following sources:

- The current running process ID

- The current thread ID

- A tick counter from since the time the machine was rebooted

- The current time

- High-precision performance counters

- A hash of user data, such as username, computer name, and so forth

- Internal high-precision timers

While all of this sounds complicated, the good news is that you don't need to understand the internal workings of any of the algorithms discussed in the book. You are not here to learn about theoretical cryptography, but to learn how to apply it in your .NET application. With that, let's look at how you generate a cryptographically secure random number using `RNGCryptoServiceProvider`.

```
using System.Security.Cryptography;

public class Random
{
    public static byte[] GenerateRandomNumber(int length)
    {
        using ( var randomNumberGenerator =
                new RNGCryptoServiceProvider())
        {
            var randomNumber = new byte[length];
            randomNumberGenerator.GetBytes(randomNumber);
            return randomNumber;
        }
    }
}
```

As you can see, making use of RNGCryptoServiceProvider is quite straightforward. The preceding method, GenerateRandomNumber, takes an integer that represents the length of the random number we want to generate. This length is the number of bytes we want to produce. If you require a 256 bit random number, then you would pass in 32, which is 32 bytes. Next, we create an instance of the RNGCryptoServiceProvider class, and then we create a new byte array that is initialized to the length we passed into the GenerateRandomNumber method. Now we call the GetBytes method on the RNGCryptoServiceProvider class instance and pass in the byte array that we just created. This fills that byte array with random data, which is then returned from the method.

That is all it takes. It is that simple. The following is a small sample program that uses the random number generator to create 20 sets of random numbers.

```
class Program
{
    static void Main(string[] args)
    {
        for (int i = 0; i < 20; i++)
        {
            string randomNumber =
                Convert.ToBase64String(
```

```
            RandomNumber.GenerateRandomNumber(32));

        Console.WriteLine(randomNumber);

    }

Console.ReadLine();
    }
}
```

The code iterates 20 times using a for loop and calls our random number generator. The random number generator returns a byte array. To display this random number on a screen (see Figure 3-1), we need to convert it to something that is more readable. To do this, we call Convert.ToBase64String, which converts the byte array into a string that we can display on the screen. There is also a method called Convert.FromBase64String, which allows you to go from a base64 string back to a byte array. This is something we will do many times throughout the book. Now that we have a working sample application, let's look at the result on the screen.

Figure 3-1. Random numbers generated with RNGCryptoServiceProvider

The random numbers we have generated are all 32 bytes in length, which is 256 bits. This is the size of the random number that we use for symmetric encryption later in the book. At a casual glance, you can see that each of the numbers is entirely different, which is what we want for effective cryptography.

Summary

Good quality, non-deterministic, random numbers are one of the essential primitives
we will look at in this book. Without genuinely random numbers, the security of
our cryptographic algorithms falls apart and becomes susceptible to attackers.
We first looked at the `System.Random` number generator in .NET, which is fine for
generating simple lottery numbers or dice rolls, but it is not suitable for cryptography
because it is not random enough. The solution recommended by Microsoft is to use
`RNGCryptoServiceProvider` because it generates higher quality, non-deterministic
numbers. In the next chapter, we look at our next cryptographic primitive, hashing,
which helps satisfy the first pillar—integrity.

CHAPTER 4

Hashing and Hashed Message Authentication Codes

Now that you know the importance of random numbers in cryptography and how to generate them, let's look at one of the pillars of cryptography. In Chapter 2, I mentioned the four pillars of modern cryptography: cryptography, integrity, authentication, and non-repudiation. In this chapter, we explore integrity and authentication by looking at the various hashing and authenticated hashing operations available in .NET. Let's start with integrity and hashing.

Hashing and Integrity

A hash function in cryptography is an algorithm that takes in a block of data and then returns a fixed-size reply, which is the (cryptographic) hash value (see Figure 4-1). Any change to the original input data results in the hash code changing. The data to be hashed is often called the *message*, and the hash value is often called the *hash code*, the *message digest*, or simply, the *digest*.

Figure 4-1. *A hash function takes data and generates a unique hash code for it*

31

© Stephen Haunts 2019
S. Haunts, *Applied Cryptography in .NET and Azure Key Vault*,
https://doi.org/10.1007/978-1-4842-4375-6_4

To be a reliable and useful hash function, it must conform to four main properties.

- The hash code must be easily calculated for any given input message.

- You should not be able to create a message that has a specified hash code.

- Any changes to the original message should completely change the hash code.

- You should not be able to find two input messages that result in the same hash code.

Another way to frame the concept of a hash function is to think of it as the digital equivalent of a fingerprint for a piece of data. Once you have generated a hash code for that piece of data, the hash code is always the same if you calculate it again, unless the original data changes in any way, no matter how small that change is.

The process of calculating a hash code or digest of an item of data is straightforward in the .NET Framework or .NET Core. There are different algorithms you can use in .NET, including MD5, SHA-1, SHA-256, and SHA-512, which we explore in this chapter.

Generating a hash code for a piece of data is a one-way operation, which means that once you have calculated the hash code for a piece of data, you cannot reverse the hash code back to the original data. There is no reversal process to return hash code back to the original data. On the flip side, encryption is designed to be a two-way operation. Once you have encrypted data with a key, you can then decrypt that data using the same key or recover the original message. Encryption is covered later in this book.

The properties of hashing, such as only being able to hash in one direction, and the hash code is unique to a piece of data, makes hashing the perfect mechanism for checking the integrity of data. Integrity checking means when you send data across a network to someone else, you can use hashing as a way to tell if the original data has been tampered with or corrupted. Before sending the data, you calculate a hash of the data to get its unique fingerprint. You then send that data and the hash to the recipient. The recipient calculates the hash of the data and then compares it to the hash you sent. If the generated hash codes are identical, then the data is successfully received without data loss or corruption. If the hash codes fail to match correctly, then the data received is not the same as the data initially sent. The two most common hashing methods are MD5 and the SHA family of hashes (SHA-1, SHA-256, and SHA-512), which are all supported in .NET. Let's look at these in more detail.

MD5

The MD5 message digest algorithm is a widely used cryptographic hash function that produces a 128-bit (16-byte) hash value, which is expressed in text format as a 32-digit hexadecimal number or as a base64-encoded string. MD5 is used in a wide variety of cryptographic applications for operating systems and large-scale enterprise systems. One of the most common uses is verifying file integrity.

MD5 was designed by Ron Rivest in 1991 to replace MD4, an earlier hash function.

A flaw in the design of MD5 was found in 1996. The flaw did not seem to be a fatal weakness, but cryptographers recommended the use of other algorithms, such as the SHA family, which we explore later in this chapter. MD5 was used commercially for a long time, but in 2004, it was discovered that MD5 is not collision-resistant, which means that it is possible that generating an MD5 hash of two sets of data could result in the same hash.

Because of this flaw, MD5 is not recommended in any new systems. It is still important to talk about its use, though, as you may still need it in applications if you are checking the integrity of data coming from a legacy system that makes use of MD5. In most companies, legacy code is something developers have to live with, which is why MD5 may still be very relevant. Old data stored in a database may contain MD5 hashes as part of the data stored in their table, and legacy code potentially checks these hashes in disparate systems. If you need to read or receive any of that data from these older systems, you need the ability to recalculate and check the same hashes.

I had this problem in a company I used to work for, which was a large Internet bank in the United Kingdom. The core banking platform lived on AS400 mainframes, and the modern website and services that the company provided were developed in .NET and ASP.NET on top of the core banking platform. This means that we frequently had to query data from the AS400 banking system. All of this data was sent with a corresponding MD5 hash of the payload, which meant to check the integrity of the financial data coming from the banking platform, we had to recalculate the MD5 hash in .NET and compare the values. If they matched, then we were happy that the data integrity was intact. The banking platform used MD5, which wasn't going to change, so we had to accept this decision and work with it. This is why MD5 is still relevant today, but don't use it unless you have to.

Creating an MD5 hash in your code is very straightforward, as you can see in the following code. In the static method, `ComputeHashMd5`, we pass in a byte array of the data we want to create a hash code for. All the hashing operations for MD5 and the SHA family of hashes work with byte arrays, so if your input data isn't in this format already, you first need to convert it; for example, if your input data is a string, then you need to use something like the `Encoding.UTF8.GetBytes` method to turn that string into an array of bytes. You see this in the example in a moment.

```
public class HashData
{
    public static byte[] ComputeHashMd5(byte[] toBeHashed)
    {
        using (var md5 = MD5.Create())
        {
            return md5.ComputeHash(toBeHashed);
        }
    }
}
```

Once you have a byte array for your data, you then need to hash it. To do this with MD5, you call the static `Create` method on the MD5 class, which gives you an instance of a class that you can use to create the hash. Once you have that instance, you call the `ComputeHash` method and pass in the byte array of the data where you want the hash code created.

Let's now look at wiring up this method and calling it. In the following sample code, we start by creating two strings containing the same text. Then we create a hash MD5 hash code for each string by first converting it to a byte array. To display the resulting hash codes onto the screen, we have to convert it from a byte array to something more display-friendly. A useful format to convert to is a base64-encoded string, which is done using the static `Convert.ToBase64String` method. Once we have done this, the hash code displays to the console window.

```
class Program
{
    static void Main()
    {
        const string originalMessage = " Message to hash";
        const string originalMessage2 = " Message to hash";

        var md5HashedMessage = HashData.ComputeHashMd5(
                Encoding.UTF8.GetBytes(originalMessage));
```

```
var md5HashedMessage2 = HashData.ComputeHashMd5(
        Encoding.UTF8.GetBytes(originalMessage2));

Console.WriteLine("Message 1 hash = " +
        Convert.ToBase64String(md5HashedMessage));

Console.WriteLine("Message 2 hash = " +
        Convert.ToBase64String(md5HashedMessage2));
}
```

As you can see, even though we were hashing to separate strings (Figure 4-2), the final hash code is the same because the strings contained the same message.

Figure 4-2. *The result of running MD5 against two identical strings*

If you were to change just a single character in one of those strings, then the generated hash codes would be completely different.

Secure Hash Algorithm (SHA) Family

MD5 shouldn't be used if you can help it, but what is the available alternative in .NET? The alternative is the Secure Hash Algorithm family of hash functions, or the SHA family. The SHA family is a family of cryptographic hash functions published by the US National Institute of Standards and Technology (NIST). The premise of the SHA family of hashes is the same as with MD5. You supply some input data, run it through the hashing function, and get a hash code back. The concept is the same, but the underlying algorithm is different, and you get a much longer and more robust hash code.

The Secure Hash family covers many variants, including the following:

- **SHA-1**. The SHA-1 hash function produces a 160-bit (20 bytes) hash code. SHA-1 was designed by the National Security Agency to be part of the Digital Signature Algorithm (DSA). Cryptographic weaknesses were discovered in SHA-1, and the standard was no longer approved for most cryptographic uses after 2010. As with MD5, it is still around to enable integration with legacy systems that use SHA-1.

- **SHA-2**. SHA-2 is a family of two similar hash functions with different block sizes known as SHA-256 and SHA-512. These hash functions differ in word size. SHA-256 uses 32-bit words, whereas SHA-512 uses 64-bit words. NSA designed these versions of the SHA algorithm.

- **SHA-3**. SHA-3 was defined after a public competition to find a hashing function implementation that was not designed by NSA. The winner was chosen in 2012. It is based on a hashing implementation called Keccak. SHA-3 supports the same hash length as SHA-2, but its internal working and structure is entirely different from SHA-1 and SHA-2. SHA-3 is not currently supported in the .NET Framework directly, although third-party implementations are available.

Implementing SHA in your applications is a straightforward process because the signatures of SHA objects are identical to those of MD5 objects. Table 4-1 shows how this is done. In the example class, we have three methods for creating our different SHA-based hashes: SHA-1, SHA-256, and SHA-512. As with the MD5 hash, the code for creating each of these hashes is almost identical; only the static hashing class names are different—SHA-1, SHA-256, and SHA-512.

Table 4-1. *Size of Hash Codes in Bits and Bytes*

Hash Type	Size in Bits	Size in Bytes
SHA-1	160	20
SHA-256	256	32
SHA-512	512	64

A SHA-1 hash returns a 160-bit or 20-byte hash code. The SHA-256 hash returns a hash code that is 256 bits or 32 bytes in length, and finally, a SHA-512 hash returns a hash code that is 512 bits or 64 bytes in length. Which type of hash function you use is a matter of preference if you need to store the hashes, but longer hash codes are more secure and resistant to hash collisions.

```
public class HashData
{
    public static byte[] ComputeHashSha1(byte[] toBeHashed)
    {
        using (var sha1 = SHA1.Create())
        {
            return sha1.ComputeHash(toBeHashed);
        }
    }

    public static byte[] ComputeHashSha256(byte[] toBeHashed)
    {
        using (var sha256 = SHA256.Create())
        {
            return sha256.ComputeHash(toBeHashed);
        }
    }

    public static byte[] ComputeHashSha512(byte[] toBeHashed)
    {
        using (var sha512 = SHA512.Create())
        {
            return sha512.ComputeHash(toBeHashed);
        }
    }
}
```

Let's now wire them up as we did with the MD5 hash example. This time, I made the two original messages different by setting originalMessage2 different by one character. Again, we need to convert the string into a byte array to calculate the hash code. Once the strings convert to a byte array, we can then calculate the hash code. When this is completed for each of our three hash types, the resulting hash code is printed to the console window by converting the hash code byte array into a base64-encoded string.

```
class Program
{
    static void Main()
    {
        const string originalMessage = "Message to hash";
        const string originalMessage2 = "M3ssage to hash";

        var sha1HashedMessage = HashData.ComputeHashSha1(
            Encoding.UTF8.GetBytes(originalMessage));
        var sha1HashedMessage2 = HashData.ComputeHashSha1(
            Encoding.UTF8.GetBytes(originalMessage2));

        var sha256HashedMessage = HashData.ComputeHashSha256(
            Encoding.UTF8.GetBytes(originalMessage));
        var sha256HashedMessage2 = HashData.ComputeHashSha256(
            Encoding.UTF8.GetBytes(originalMessage2));

        var sha512HashedMessage = HashData.ComputeHashSha512(
            Encoding.UTF8.GetBytes(originalMessage));
        var sha512HashedMessage2 = HashData.ComputeHashSha512(
            Encoding.UTF8.GetBytes(originalMessage2));

        Console.WriteLine();
        Console.WriteLine("SHA 1 Hashes");
        Console.WriteLine("Message 1 hash = " +
            Convert.ToBase64String(sha1HashedMessage));
        Console.WriteLine("Message 2 hash = " +
            Convert.ToBase64String(sha1HashedMessage2));
        Console.WriteLine();

        Console.WriteLine("SHA 256 Hashes");
        Console.WriteLine("Message 1 hash = " +
            Convert.ToBase64String(sha256HashedMessage));
        Console.WriteLine("Message 2 hash = " +
            Convert.ToBase64String(sha256HashedMessage2));
        Console.WriteLine();

        Console.WriteLine("SHA 512 Hashes");
        Console.WriteLine("Message 1 hash = " +
```

```
                Convert.ToBase64String(sha512HashedMessage));
            Console.WriteLine("Message 2 hash = " +
                Convert.ToBase64String(sha512HashedMessage2));
        }
    }
```

When you look at the output of this example in the console window (Figure 4-3), you can see the difference in the size of the final base64 string. The SHA-512 hash is double the size of the SHA-256 hash. If you are not storing many hashes, then you may want to go straight to SHA-512. SHA-512 hashes provide the best security and future proofing. If you are storing many hashes and you feel storage double the size of the hash string is an issue, then a SHA-256 hash is a reasonable default.

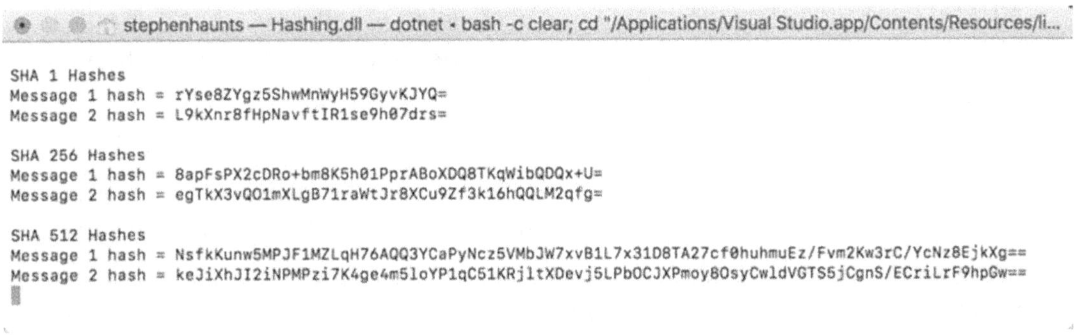
stephenhaunts — Hashing.dll — dotnet • bash -c clear; cd "/Applications/Visual Studio.app/Contents/Resources/li...
SHA 1 Hashes
Message 1 hash = rYse8ZYgz5ShwMnWyH59GyvKJYQ=
Message 2 hash = L9kXnr8fHpNavftIR1se9h07drs=
SHA 256 Hashes
Message 1 hash = 8apFsPX2cDRo+bm8K5h01PprABoXDQ8TKqWibQDQx+U=
Message 2 hash = egTkX3vQO1mXLgB71raWtJr8XCu9Zf3k16hQQLM2qfg=
SHA 512 Hashes
Message 1 hash = NsfkKunw5MPJF1MZLqH76AQQ3YCaPyNcz5VMbJW7xvB1L7x31D8TA27cf0huhmuEz/Fvm2Kw3rC/YcNz8EjkXg==
Message 2 hash = keJiXhJI2iNPMPzi7K4ge4m5loYP1qC51KRjltXDevj5LPbOCJXPmoy8OsyCwldVGTS5jCgnS/ECriLrF9hpGw==

Figure 4-3. *The result of running SHA family hashes against two different strings*

We now have the ability to perform integrity checking through hashing. Let's extend this capability with authentication by looking at hashed message authentication codes.

Authenticated Hashing

So far, we have covered MD5 and the SHA family of hashing functions. Their purpose is to provide integrity checking capabilities within applications to help detect if data has been tampered with or corrupted over time. What we want to do now is satisfy another of our four pillars of cryptography by talking about authentication, which naturally follows integrity.

If you combine a one-way hash function with a secret cryptographic key (Figure 4-4), you get a *hash message authentication code* (HMAC). Like a hash code, a HMAC verifies the integrity of a message.

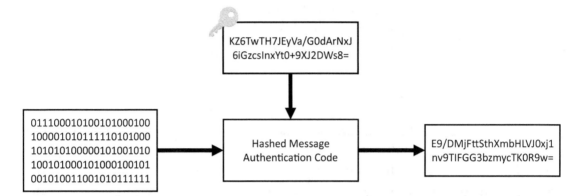

Figure 4-4. *HMAC is similar to a normal hashing function, except that it takes a key as well as its input data*

A HMAC also allows you to verify the authentication of a message, because only the person who knows the key can calculate the same message's hash. Let's walk through that with an example.

Let's say you have a PDF file on your computer, and you calculate an HMAC of that data. To do this, you create a key using the same technique we talked about in Chapter 3. You generate a 256-bit or 32-byte random number using the RNGCryptoServiceProvider class. You take the PDF file and the key, pass it in the HMAC function, and get a hash code back. You then send the PDF to a colleague along with the key. (We won't worry about how you send the key just yet because we tackle that problem later in the book.) Your colleague recalculates the hash code using the same key, and they receive the same hash code in response, which means they are confident that the PDF file is intact.

The same day, someone else gets hold of a copy of the PDF file and tries to calculate the same hash code. The problem is they do not have a copy of the key, so when they try to recalculate the hash code, they get a completely different response; the hash code doesn't match for this person because they are not in possession of the correct key. This means that only the authorized person can calculate the same hash code for a file. The authorized party has a copy of the correct key.

Why does this matter so much? Well, it gives us a level of trust. If Alice and Bob are the only people who know the authentication key for the HMAC; if Alice sends Bob a message and a hash code, when Bob recalculates the hash (with the key he has), if the hashes match, Bob is confident that that data came from Alice. On the flipside to that, if our hacker, Eve, sends a message to Bob but uses a different key; when Bob recalculates the hash with the key he knows Alice has, the hash codes won't match. If they don't match, he shouldn't trust the message that has been sent to him and Bob should disregard it.

I'll summarize the fundamental differences between a standard MD5 or SHA hash and an HMAC: anyone can calculate a hash code using MD5 or SHA and get the same results for a piece of data. Only an authorized individual can generate the same hash code using an HMAC because they need to have the same key used to generate the original HMAC hash code.

A HMAC, while requiring a key to be passed in, can be used with different hashing functions like MD5 or the SHA family of algorithms. The cryptographic strength of an HMAC depends on the size of the key that is used for the hash. When I use a HMAC in the systems I develop, I tend to use a 32-byte random number. Another common way to provide a key is a standard password that is first hashed with SHA-256, and then the hashed password is used as the key. If you need an ordinary person to provide a key, then using passwords is common, but then you have the problem of weak passwords to deal with. I talk about passwords and password storage in the next chapter.

The most common attack against an HMAC is a brute-force attack to uncover the key. A brute-force attack involves trying multiple combinations of a key until you find the correct key. The attacker tries to find a new key by iterating in a loop, and then compares the hash code output with the original hash code. This is why using a secure key such as a 32-byte randomly generated key is better; the chances of finding the correct key are significantly harder.

Passwords, on the other hand, are much easier to crack because the attacker can use a *dictionary attack* to recover the password. This is where a vast precomputed list of passwords and their corresponding hashes are stored. The attacker then checks to see if the hash code for the key is in the dictionary. If it is, they know the key. The dictionaries contain several gigabytes of precomputed passwords, including all the common variants in which people switch vowels into numbers or insert an exclamation mark at the end of the password.

Earlier I said that one of the requirements for a hashing algorithm is to not produce a hash code that is the same for two different pieces of original data, which is called a *hash collision*. Hash collisions are one of the main reasons why MD5 is no longer recommended. HMACs are substantially less affected by hash collisions than their underlying hashing algorithms, such as MD5 or SHA, because you are also using a key to add entropy to the source data being hashed.

In the following example, we look at how to use the different HMAC variants available in .NET. First, we have a class called Hmac. This class has everything needed to perform a hashed message authentication code, including the generation of a random number key. The code in GenerateKey is identical to the random number generator we used in

Chapter 3. In this example, we use RNGCryptoServiceProvider to generate a fixed-size 32 byte or 256 bit key. The key doesn't have to be this size, but I always default to 32 bytes because it is more impervious to a brute-force attack. You can make the key longer if you wish, or you can make it shorter, but personally, I wouldn't go shorter than 32 bytes.

Next, we have the code to generate an HMAC based on the SHA-256 algorithm. First, an instance of the HMACSHA256 class is instantiated with the key passed into the constructor. Next, you call ComputeHash by passing in a byte array of the data you want hashed. Again, if your data is not represented as a byte array, you need to convert it. When ComputeHash finishes, it returns a byte array with the final hash code. The fundamental difference from ordinary hashing is that this hash is dependent on the key that is generated, so if the recipient of the hash wants to calculate the same hash code for the same input data, they need a copy of that key.

The process for calculating SHA-1, SHA-512, or MD5-based HMACs is the same, except the classes that you instantiate with the key as the constructor parameter are different. The classes are HMACSHA1, HMACSHA256, HMACSHA512, and HMACMD5, respectively.

```
public class Hmac
{
    private const int KeySize = 32;

    public static byte[] GenerateKey()
    {
        using (var randomNumberGenerator =
                    new RNGCryptoServiceProvider())
        {
            var randomNumber = new byte[KeySize];
            randomNumberGenerator.GetBytes(randomNumber);

            return randomNumber;
        }
    }

    public static byte[] ComputeHmacsha256(byte[] toBeHashed, byte[] key)
    {
        using (var hmac = new HMACSHA256(key))
        {
            return hmac.ComputeHash(toBeHashed);
        }
```

```
    }

    public static byte[] ComputeHmacsha1(byte[] toBeHashed, byte[] key)
    {
        using (var hmac = new HMACSHA1(key))
        {
            return hmac.ComputeHash(toBeHashed);
        }
    }

    public static byte[] ComputeHmacsha512(byte[] toBeHashed, byte[] key)
    {
        using (var hmac = new HMACSHA512(key))
        {
            return hmac.ComputeHash(toBeHashed);
        }
    }

    public static byte[] ComputeHmacmd5(byte[] toBeHashed, byte[] key)
    {
        using (var hmac = new HMACMD5(key))
        {
            return hmac.ComputeHash(toBeHashed);
        }
    }
}
```

We now have a helper class that can calculate HMACs and generate our key. Let's hook them up to see an example. In our Main method, we first declare a const string with the string that we want to calculate the HMAC. Then we generate our key using our help method, GenerateKey. Next, calculate the HMACs of our test string using the key. HMACS are calculated using the MD5, SHA-1, SHA-256, and SHA-512 variants by first converting our sample string into a byte array. Once the HMACs are calculated, they are converted to base64-encoded strings. Then the result is output to the console display.

```
class Program
{
    static void Main()
    {
        const string originalMessage = "Message to hash";

        var key = Hmac.GenerateKey();

        var hmacMd5Message = Hmac.ComputeHmacmd5(
            Encoding.UTF8.GetBytes(originalMessage), key);

        var hmacSha1Message = Hmac.ComputeHmacsha1(
            Encoding.UTF8.GetBytes(originalMessage), key);

        var hmacSha256Message = Hmac.ComputeHmacsha256(
            Encoding.UTF8.GetBytes(originalMessage), key);

        var hmacSha512Message = Hmac.ComputeHmacsha512(
            Encoding.UTF8.GetBytes(originalMessage), key);

        Console.WriteLine();
        Console.WriteLine("MD5 HMAC");
        Console.WriteLine("hash = " +
                Convert.ToBase64String(hmacMd5Message));

        Console.WriteLine();
        Console.WriteLine("SHA 1 HMAC");
        Console.WriteLine("hash = " +
                Convert.ToBase64String(hmacSha1Message));

        Console.WriteLine();
        Console.WriteLine("SHA 256 HMAC");
        Console.WriteLine("hash = " +
                Convert.ToBase64String(hmacSha256Message));

        Console.WriteLine();
        Console.WriteLine("SHA 512 HMAC");
```

```
        Console.WriteLine("hash = " +
                Convert.ToBase64String(hmacSha512Message));
    }
}
```

The result of this sample application is shown in Figure 4-5. As with standard hashing, you can see the difference in size between the resulting hash codes.

```
●  ●  ●  ⌂ stephenhaunts — HMAC.dll — dotnet ‹ bash -c clear; cd "/Applications/Visual Studio.app/Contents/Resources/lib/mono...

MD5 HMAC
hash = W+WPTBJyPIRIJXFgCfz98g==

SHA 1 HMAC
hash = ukMm4eV7DjCpNwVIbjKkf8Iiubk=

SHA 256 HMAC
hash = 1G2PoE6nYHAUyKw7aYrzfN9DNRZBsS6I1K4A6wZJdnU=

SHA 512 HMAC
hash = SFlklIqJU5jblVnra74FbI+iuYcxZjHzX7PJdK6/4j5v2DkyZZWF0oHvB3//yxuUgpcomDRQUny2tNoJ5UW59g==
```

Figure 4-5. *The result of running HMACs for our input data with a precomputed key*

Summary

In this chapter, we explored classes in .NET to help satisfy two of the four pillars of cryptography: integrity and authentication. We used hashing algorithms such as MD5 and the SHA family of hashes to accomplish our integrity checking. The benefit of integrity checking is that if you're sending data to another system or person, you can calculate a hash code of that data before sending it. The recipient can then recalculate the hash code from the data they receive and compare it to the original hash code sent to them. If they match, then the data wasn't tampered with or corrupted.

Hashing functions, such as MD5 and the SHA hashes, work by passing source data into the hashing function, and then getting a unique hash code returned for that data. It should not be possible to produce the same hash for two different pieces of source data; if you encounter this, it is called a hash collision. MD5 is susceptible to this problem, which is why it is not recommended to use it in new applications. We covered how to use MD5 because you will most likely need it when interfacing with legacy systems. The recommendation is to use the SHA family of hashes, ideally SHA-256.

Then, I introduced authentication. Hashed message authentication codes, or HMACs for short, extend the hashing concept by providing a key as well as the original data that you want to hash. This gives us a unique property in that the recipient can only recalculate the same hash for some data if they are in possession of the key. If they don't have the key or an incorrect key, then the resulting hash code will be different. This has another unique property in that if the recipient can recalculate the correct hash code with their key, then they have a level of confidence that the correct person sent the message. If an imposter sent the message and hash code, they would have a different key, provider the originator had kept their key safe. I cover the safe storage of keys later in the book.

In the next chapter, we build upon what we have covered in this chapter by talking about secure password storage.

CHAPTER 5

Safely Storing Passwords

Now that we have covered hashing and authenticated hashing, the next place to explore is the protection and storage of passwords. Passwords are still the most common way to authenticate a user, but it is easy to put yourself in a situation where your system is not secure and is susceptible to attacks.

This chapter discusses ways in which you shouldn't store passwords, and then talks about how you can safely store passwords and protect yourself from being a victim of data theft.

I start by discussing techniques that you shouldn't use and gradually move to a better solution.

In this chapter, we look at

- Storing passwords in the clear

- Encrypting passwords

- Using hashes to store passwords

- Using salted hashes to store passwords

- Using password-based key derivation functions

First, let's take a look at storing passwords in the clear.

Storing Passwords in the Clear

When you are working to create a system that needs to authenticate a user with passwords you need to store those passwords somewhere so that the user can come back later to log in. There are lots of techniques that you can use to store the password, but by far the biggest mistake you can make is to store passwords as cleartext in your database. To do so counteracts the very benefit of having passwords in the first place, which is to authenticate and grant access to a system using a password known only by the user.

© Stephen Haunts 2019

S. Haunts, *Applied Cryptography in .NET and Azure Key Vault*,
https://doi.org/10.1007/978-1-4842-4375-6_5

Although a system needs to be able to verify a password, the system should never need to want or know the actual password.

The significant risk here is that if your database is compromised and the password tables are stolen, the attacker doesn't have to do any hard work to gain access to your customers' accounts. They log in with the user-name and passwords that were stolen from your database. This could have catastrophic consequences for your business.

Having customer accounts compromised means that your customers could not only lose out financially, but they lose trust in your system, and your organization could suffer much reputational damage. Compromised accounts could not only open you up to many lawsuits as people sue your company, especially if your company's lax security has defrauded the customer, but it could drive customers away from you to a competitor, and you eventually lose market share in your particular market.

If you work in a regulated environment, your company could face very high fines for not protecting customer or user data adequately, which includes insufficient storage of a user's credentials.

So, we have determined that storing plaintext passwords is a terrible idea.

Now let's look at some better options. First, let's cover encrypting passwords.

Encrypting Passwords

We are covering encryption and decryption in more detail later on in this book, but I want to talk about encryption with regards to password storage early. Encryption is a two-way process; you encrypt using a secret key and can then decrypt with the same key. This mechanism could be used to store passwords, and it is indeed much better than storing passwords in the clear, but this approach comes with its own set of problems and challenges.

- First, you have to manage the keys.

- Encryption keys need to be stored somewhere.

- What do you do if those keys are compromised?

- How do you effectively share that key with other people?

- Does every client application need access to the key to encrypt a password before sending it to the server?

As you can see, this throws up lots of questions and challenges, with key management the hardest to solve. Instead of using a symmetric key encryption algorithm like what we will look at later in this book, you could use an Asymmetric Encryption algorithm like RSA, where the client only needs to use a public key. I cover this in more detail later, but for the sake of the conversation about storing passwords, this is still not a great solution due to the complexities of key management.

Will you need to decrypt the password?

Would you ever need to see what it is?

The answers should be no, as having the ability to decrypt the password coupled with the complexities of key management is not a good solution that opens you up to many vulnerabilities. If an attacker gets a copy of the decryption key and your password table, they have access to everything. You then need to change the encryption key and prompt all of your users to change their passwords, so they are re-encrypted; this is not a good situation to be faced with.

So, what can we do instead?

Instead of using a two-way encryption process to hide passwords, we can use a one-way system using hashing as discussed in Chapter 3, but there are good ways and bad ways of doing this.

Using Hashes to Store Passwords

Storing passwords in the clear in a database is not a good idea. Encrypting passwords is a better solution, but there should be no need to reverse an encrypted password to plaintext, and the overhead of key management makes this a pretty complicated solution.

Instead of encrypting the passwords, we look at hashing them. Hashing is a one-way function, which means that once you have hashed the password, you shouldn't be able to reverse the hash back to the original password. Cryptographic hashing has four main properties, as introduced in Chapter 4.

- It is easy to compute the hash value for any given message.

- It is infeasible to generate a message that has a given hash.

- It is infeasible to modify a message without changing the hash.

- It is infeasible to find two different messages with the same hash.

These properties make hashing a much better solution for encoding the password before storage as the hashing process is natural to perform, yet harder to go from the hash back to the password. While hashing the password with an algorithm like MD5, SHA-1, or SHA-2 seems like a much better solution, it does have some shortcomings.

Hashing the password is susceptible to two different attacks. They are a brute-force attack and a rainbow table attack (see Figure 5-1). A brute-force attack is where the attacker tries different combinations of passwords until they get one that matches a password hash; this is easier if the attacker has already compromised your hashed password tables from your database. They can have an extensive dictionary of passwords already prepared and the compromised passwords through this dictionary until they find a match against a hash in your password table.

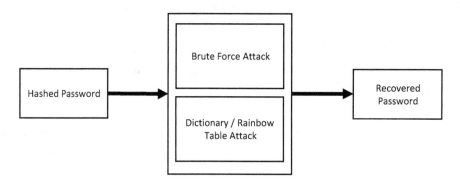

Figure 5-1. *Performing attacks against a hash's password*

To try and make passwords stronger people tend to try adding in different characters like turning vowels into a number in the hope that this makes their passwords stronger, but it doesn't take much work to make a dictionary attack try different combinations of a word with these various letter substitutions.

It may sound like a lot of work to break a password, but with the advent of modern processors and graphical processing units (GPUs), it is possible for an attacker to try tens of billions of passwords every second. It is only a matter of time until they get the correct password. Unfortunately, people still tend to pick weak passwords based on names or other simple words, so the brute-force process is remarkably effective.

An alternative attack from a brute-force attack is that of using a rainbow table. A rainbow table contains an extensive dictionary of precomputed hashes for different passwords. These tables are used to determine the original plain-text from an already computed password hash value. Rainbow tables can be many gigabytes in size and they significantly speed up attacks to recover the original value of a hash.

A better approach to straight hashing is to increase the entropy of the password being attacked by making the password harder to recover. Entropy is the measure of a password's strength and how easy it is to guess it. If you extend a password with additional random letters and numbers, then this is much harder to guess; this is done by adding a salt value to the password before hashing (see Figure 5-2).

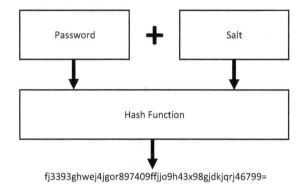

fj3393ghwej4jgor897409ffjjo9h43x98gjdkjqrj46799=

Figure 5-2. *Salting a password before hashing*

The salt can be generated as a random number and then appended on the password before hashing. By adding a salt value, you are making the password a lot more complicated, and this makes a brute force or rainbow table attach much harder to achieve.

When you store the hashed password and salt, you do not need to treat the salt as a secret entity. It is okay to include the salt value along with the hashed password in the database; this is because the salt is not considered an encryption key. The main benefit of a salt, provided you use a different salt per password, is that the resulting hash is different for each user if they have the same password.

Let's look at some sample code for performing a salted hash of a password.

First, we have a class called Hash. This class contains all we need to perform a self-contained salted hash of some data. There is a method to generate our salt called GenerateSalt. This method uses the RNGCryptoServiceProvider object that we explored earlier in this book; the only difference is that we are generating a fixed size of 32 bytes for our random number instead of letting the caller pass in the size value.

The next method in this class is called Combine. The purpose of this method is to combine two bytes arrays into a single byte array, which is used to add our pre-generated salt onto the password that we wish to hash. Finally, there is a method called HashPasswordWithSalt that takes byte arrays for the password to be hashed and the salt that has been generated. In this method, the SHA-256 object is first created, and then the salt and password arrays are combined before calculating the final hash, which is returned as a byte array. When this hashed password is stored in a database (after being converted to a base64 string), you also need to store a version of the salt; otherwise, you will not be able to calculate the same hash again.

```
public class Hash
{
    public static byte[] GenerateSalt()
    {
        const int saltLength = 32;

        using (var randomNumberGenerator =
                    new RNGCryptoServiceProvider())
        {
            var randomNumber = new byte[saltLength];
            randomNumberGenerator.GetBytes(randomNumber);

            return randomNumber;
        }
    }

    private static byte[] Combine(byte[] first, byte[] second)
    {
        var ret = new byte[first.Length + second.Length];

        Buffer.BlockCopy(first, 0, ret, 0, first.Length);

        Buffer.BlockCopy(second, 0, ret, first.Length,
                        second.Length);

        return ret;
    }

    public static byte[] HashPasswordWithSalt(
                            byte[] toBeHashed, byte[] salt)
    {
        using (var sha256 = SHA256.Create())
        {
            return sha256.ComputeHash(Combine(toBeHashed,
                                    salt));
        }
    }
}
```

Now that we have all the components to create our salted hash, let's connect them. The sample application starts by defining a password as a string. Then the salt is generated and stored in a byte array. Then the password hash is calculated by passing in the password (which first has to be converted into a byte array), and the salt; this results in a final hash of the password and the salt combined. The hashed password is then converted to a base64 string and then printed to the console. If you are going to store the password, then converting to base64 makes storage much easier. You must also store the salt in your database as it is needed to recalculate the hash.

```
class Program
{
    static void Main()
    {
        const string password = "V3ryCOmpl3xP455wOrd";
        byte[] salt = Hash.GenerateSalt();

        Console.WriteLine("Password : " + password);
        Console.WriteLine("Salt = " +
                Convert.ToBase64String(salt));
        Console.WriteLine();

        var hashedPassword1 = Hash.HashPasswordWithSalt(
            Encoding.UTF8.GetBytes(password),
            salt);

        Console.WriteLine("Hashed Password = " +
                Convert.ToBase64String(hashedPassword1));

        Console.ReadLine();
    }
}
```

The screenshot in Figure 5-3 shows the results of running this sample application. Salted hashes have been a conventional technique for hashing and storing passwords for many years, but you can go one step further to create securer passwords.

```
stephenhaunts — HashPassword.dll — dotnet • bash -c clear; cd "/Application...

Password : V3ryC0mpl3xP455w0rd
Salt = GKOJeqb5JqiNa6nhdgf8WGrW/NEU8gXK98lHdBbuHtk=

Hashed Password = gSvRAE1BycvRUtpkWlQ740SNtF54AT01W1iE34RENew=
```

Figure 5-3. *Result of a salted password hash*

This next technique is called a *password-based key derivation function*; let's explore this in more detail.

Using Password Based Key Derivation Functions

The problem with storing passwords and hashing them (even with a salt value) is that as microprocessors and graphics processors get faster, we run the risk of what we currently think are secure passwords being compromised because processors can perform brute-force attacks and rainbow table attacks faster. What we need is a solution that allows us to hash our passwords with a salt value still but help us guard against advancements in Moore's law.

Moore's law (named after Gordon E. Moore, the cofounder of Intel) states that the number of transistors in a circuit doubles approximately every two years. This means that as processors become faster and more powerful, what may be a robust password against a brute-force attack today, eventually becomes a very easy password because more combinations are tried in a shorter space of time. The solution is a password-based key derivation function, or PBKDF2.

A PBKDF2 is part of the RSA Public Key Cryptographic Standards series (PKCS #5 version 2.0). PBKDF2 is also part of the Internet Engineering Task Force's RFC2898 specification.

A password-based key derivation function takes a password, a salt (to add additional entropy to the password) and a "number of iterations" value (see Figure 5-4). The number of iterations value repeats the hash operation over the password multiple times to produce a derived key for the password that can be stored in a database.

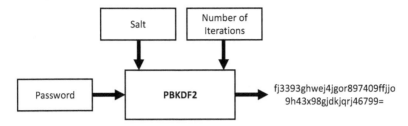

Figure 5-4. *Password-based key derivation*

By iterating a hash process over the password multiple times, you are slowing down the hashing process algorithmically, which makes brute force or dictionary table attacks against the password much harder to perform; this means that fewer passwords can be tested at once.

As computer processors and GPU's get faster over time, you can increase the number of iterations used to create the new password, which means a password-based key derivation function can scale with Moore's law. A reasonable default to start with for the number of iterations is around 150,000. You need to pick a number of iterations or work factor that is suitable for your own circumstances. For example, if you are using the PBKDF2 as part of a user authenticating with your system, then you need to ask yourself, is the additional delay encountered should be acceptable? Hopefully, it is.

It is a good practice to increase the work factor, preferably, by doubling, at least every two years. You can manage this as part of your standard password updating process. If you force your staff or customers to update their password every three months, then you can design your system, from a specific point in time when the new password is hashed and stored, and use a stronger work factor.

By adding a salt value to the derivation function, you further reduce the ability of a rainbow table to recover the original password. A reasonable minimum length for your salt is at least 64 bits (8 bytes), but in our demo, in a moment we use a 256-bit (32-byte) salt.

The .NET object we use to perform the key derivation function is Rfc2898DeriveBytes. Let's run through a sample application that uses this password-based key derivation function.

```
public class PBKDF2
{
    public static byte[] GenerateSalt()
    {
        using (var randomNumberGenerator =
                    new RNGCryptoServiceProvider())
```

```
        {
            var randomNumber = new byte[32];
            randomNumberGenerator.GetBytes(randomNumber);

            return randomNumber;
        }
    }

    public static byte[] HashPassword(byte[] toBeHashed,
                            byte[] salt, int numberOfRounds)
    {
        using (var rfc2898 = new Rfc2898DeriveBytes(
                            toBeHashed, salt, numberOfRounds))
        {
            return rfc2898.GetBytes(20);
        }
    }
}
```

Although the term *password-based key derivation function* makes the technique sound complicated, the reality is far from that. In our example class called PBKDF2, we first have a method called GenerateSalt. This method is precisely the same as what appeared in the salted hash demo earlier in the chapter in that it uses RNGCryptoServiceProvider to generate a fixed length 32-byte array.

Next, we have the HashPassword method, which takes as its input a byte array of the password to hash, a byte array of the salt, and finally an integer for the number of rounds or iterations we want the key derivation function to use.

These three pieces of data are then passed into a new instance of Rfc2898DeriveBytes to create the hashed password. When GetBytes is called to extract the hash, notice we only get 20 bytes; this is because the underlying hashing function inside Rfc2898DeriveBytes uses the SHA-1 algorithm to produce the hash. SHA-1 produces a 160-bit or 20-byte hash code.

Let's hook all this up into a sample application with the following code. The example hashes the password several times using different iteration values. The actual hashing takes place in the HashPassword method. This method also sets up a stopwatch to time the hashing process. The resulting hash (in base64 format) and timings are displayed to the console so that you can see the relationship between the number of iterations and the time taken to complete the hash.

```
class Program
{
    static void Main()
    {
        const string passwordToHash = "VeryComplexPassword";

        HashPassword(passwordToHash, 100);
        HashPassword(passwordToHash, 1000);
        HashPassword(passwordToHash, 10000);
        HashPassword(passwordToHash, 50000);
        HashPassword(passwordToHash, 100000);
        HashPassword(passwordToHash, 200000);
        HashPassword(passwordToHash, 1500000);

        Console.ReadLine();
    }

    private static void HashPassword(string passwordToHash,
                                     int numberOfRounds)
    {
        var sw = new Stopwatch();

        sw.Start();

        var hashedPassword = PBKDF2.HashPassword(
                    Encoding.UTF8.GetBytes(passwordToHash),
                    PBKDF2.GenerateSalt(),
                    numberOfRounds);

        sw.Stop();

        Console.WriteLine();
        Console.WriteLine("Password to hash : " + passwordToHash);
```

```
Console.WriteLine("Hashed Password : " +
            Convert.ToBase64String(hashedPassword));

Console.WriteLine("Iterations <" + numberOfRounds + ">
            Elapsed Time : " +
            sw.ElapsedMilliseconds + "ms");
    }
}
```

You can see the result of running this sample application in the console screenshot shown in Figure 5-5.

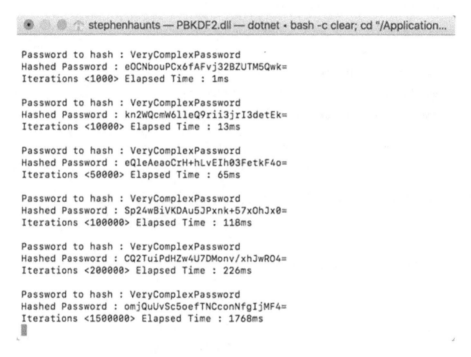

Figure 5-5. *Running PBKDF2 hashing with variable iterations*

Increasing the iteration count means the hashing process takes longer. But what is the correlation between the number of iterations passed in and the time taken? As you can see in Table 5-1, the more iterations that you perform, the longer the hash takes to calculate.

Table 5-1. *Example PBKDF2 Timings*

Number of Iterations	Time (ms)
100	0
1000	1
10,000	13
50,000	65
100,000	118
200,000	226
500,000	950

When you plot these onto a graph, you can see the rate of growth in the time taken as the number of iterations increases (see Figure 5-6).

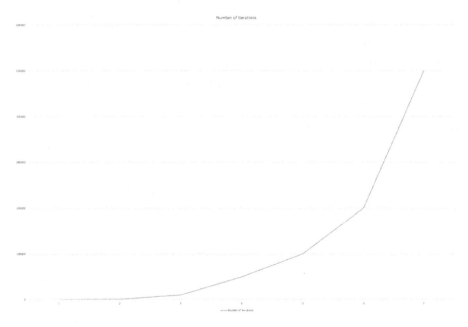

Figure 5-6. *PBKDF2 timings plotted on a graph*

If you store passwords, then typically you use them as an authentication measure into your system. You need to trade off the amount of time it takes to calculate the hash by using the PBKDF2 against the responsiveness of someone logging into your system, as you need to recalculate the hash to make sure it matches the password hash sent to you. The more iterations that you use, the slower this will be.

Summary

Securely storing passwords is an essential task for any system, yet so many companies don't do an outstanding job at it. There are, unfortunately, still systems that use plaintext passwords. Thankfully, this number is going doing down, but they do still exist. A better solution, although not perfect, is to use hashing to protect your passwords, preferably a stronger hash like SHA-256. While this is a much better solution than plaintext, it is still susceptible to brute force or dictionary table attacks. As computers and GPUs get more powerful, what may have been a securely hashed password today, can be quickly recovered in a few years' time.

An even better solution to straight hashing is salted hashing, which is where you increase the entropy of the original password by generating a random number that you append to the password before hashing. You need to store this salt value, but the salting process makes brute forcing and rainbow tables significantly more complicated to perform; this is a good solution and one that is used by many companies today, but there is a better solution. That better solution is to use a *password-based key derivation function*, or a PBKDF2, as it is also known. The PBKDF2 process is similar to the salted hash technique, but it introduces an extra input into the function, which is a number of iterations count. The purpose of this count is to algorithmically slow down the hashing process to make brute-force attacks harder. Instead of modern GPUs attempting billions of hashes per second, a password-based key derivation function like could reduce the number of attempts so five or ten hashes per second. This makes the password cracking process more robust and more secure.

You need to be mindful of the number that you use for the iteration count; for example, if you use the PBKDF2 process to protect the logon passwords for your website, the delay caused by the iterated hash will cause a noticeable delay when the user tries to log on to your site. A delay is inevitable, but you need to put some thought into it first.

CHAPTER 6

Symmetric Encryption

So far, we have covered integrity by looking at hashing, and authentication by looking at hashed message authentication codes. In this chapter, we explore confidentiality by looking at symmetric encryption.

First, we look at the history of the Data Encryption Standard (DES) and its immediate successor, Triple DES. While DES and Triple DES are not recommended for use in new applications, it is still necessary to discuss them because you may need to integrate with legacy systems that still rely on them. Once we cover DES and Triple DES, we take a look at their successor, the Advanced Encryption Standard.

This chapter isn't meant to be an advanced analysis of these algorithms at an advanced mathematical level because you don't need to understand how these algorithms work to use them entirely, but a little background information sets some useful context when using them in your applications. Once you have foundational knowledge of how these algorithms work, we look at their implementations within the .NET Framework and .NET Core.

Symmetric Encryption

In the last chapter, we discussed how hashing and hashed message authentication codes are one-way operations. Once you hash some data, you shouldn't be able to reverse the hash to go back to the original data. Symmetric encryption algorithms, on the other hand, are a two-way operation where you use the same key for both encryption and decryption of your message (see Figure 6-1). You can reverse the encryption process to recover the original data (provided that you use the same key), which is why it is referred to as *symmetric*.

© Stephen Haunts 2019
S. Haunts, *Applied Cryptography in .NET and Azure Key Vault*,
https://doi.org/10.1007/978-1-4842-4375-6_6

Figure 6-1. *Symmetric encryption uses the same key for encryption and decryption*

Symmetric encryption has both advantages and disadvantages to its use.

Advantage: Very Secure

When using a secure algorithm such as AES, symmetric encryption is exceptionally secure. One of the most widely used symmetric key encryption systems is the U.S. government-designated Advanced Encryption Standard. As of the writing of this book, AES is unbroken, so it is one of the recommended algorithms.

Advantage: Fast

One of the current problems with public key encryption systems (such as RSA which we explore in Chapter 7) is that they need complicated mathematics to work, making them very computationally intensive and slow. Encrypting and decrypting symmetric key data is easier to do, giving you excellent read and write performance. In fact, many solid-state drives, which are very fast, use symmetric key encryption store data, yet they are still a lot faster than unencrypted standard hard drives.

Disadvantage: Sharing Keys Is Hard

One of the most significant problems with symmetric key encryption algorithms is that you need to have a way to get the key to the person with who you are sending the encrypted data. Encryption keys aren't simple strings of text like passwords; they are byte arrays of randomly generated data, such as the random numbers we generated with `RNGCryptoServiceProvider` earlier in this book. As such, you'll need to have a safe way to get the key to the other person.

Symmetric key encryption is particularly useful when encrypting your information as opposed to when sharing encrypted information. There are ways to use the power of symmetric encryption with a suitable key sharing scheme, which we look at later in the book when I talk about hybrid encryption schemes.

Disadvantage: Dangerous If Compromised

When someone gets hold of one of your symmetric keys, they can decrypt everything encrypted with that key. When you're using symmetric encryption for two-way communications, this means that both sides of the conversation get compromised. With asymmetrical public-key cryptography like RSA, someone that gets your private key can decrypt messages sent to you but can't decrypt what you send to the other party since that is encrypted with a different key pair.

History of DES and Triple DES

The Data Encryption Standard, or DES, was created in the early 1970s at IBM, and later, in 1977, the algorithm was submitted to the National Bureau of Standards (NBS) to be approved as Federal Information Processing Standard 46 (FIPS 46).

With consultation from the National Security Agency (NSA), the National Bureau of Standards accepted a slightly modified version of DES as the standard FIPS 46 in the same year to provide security for the unclassified electronic data of the U.S. government.

The data is encrypted in DES using 64-bit blocks, where the input data to be encrypted is split into 64-bit (8-byte) chunks, which are encrypted using a 56-bit symmetric key to provide confidentiality and privacy (see Figure 6-2). Although DES is not the recommended standard for encryption these days, there are still a lot of legacy systems that use DES, especially in mainframe banking applications; this makes looking at DES still relevant for discussion in this course, because you may have to maintain or integrate with older systems that encrypt their data with DES.

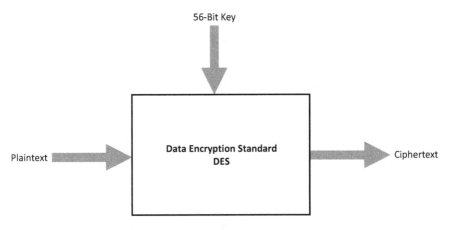

Figure 6-2. *DES uses a short 56-bit key*

The original DES cipher's key size of 56 bits was sufficient when the algorithm was designed, but the availability of increasing computational power made brute-force attacks more feasible.

There were several projects to try and break DES. The most well-known is the DESCHALL Project. If you want to read more about how it was done, and it is a fascinating story, then I recommend you read the book *Brute Force: Cracking the Data Encryption Standard* by Matt Curtin (Copernicus Books, 2005).

Once DES was compromised, a new variant was put into action called Triple DES. Triple DES represented an easy way of increasing the key size of DES to protect against such attacks, without the need to design an entirely new block cipher algorithm. Many former DES users now use Triple DES. Triple DES involves applying DES three times with two or three different keys. Triple DES is regarded as adequately secure, although it is quite slow. In Figure 6-3, you can see that three instances of DES are set to run in series.

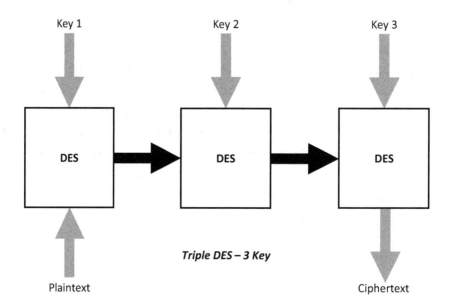

Figure 6-3. *The three-key variant of Triple DES*

The plaintext is first encrypted with Key 1.

The output of this encryption is then encrypted with Key 2.

Then the result of the data encrypted with Key 2 is then encrypted with Key 3.

This then gives you your final encrypted ciphertext.

To go from ciphertext back to the original plaintext you run the process in reverse. Another variation of Triple DES is the two-key version shown in Figure 6-4.

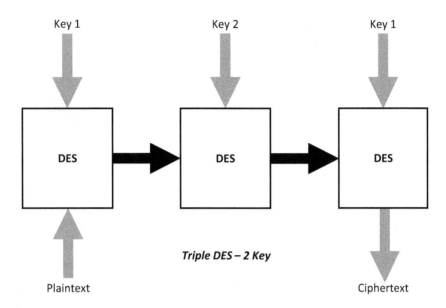

Figure 6-4. *The two-key variant of Triple DES*

In this version, the plaintext is encrypted with Key 1.

The output of this encryption is then re-encrypted using Key 2.

Then the output of this is re-encrypted with Key 1.

The three-key variant of DES offers the best security for this algorithm with a total key length of 168 bits. The two-key variant offers a compromise on key length (112 bits) between the original DES and the three-key variant.

How DES and Triple DES Works

The internal structure of DES is called a block cipher, an algorithm that takes a fixed-length stream of plaintext bytes and processes them through a series of operations into a ciphertext byte stream of the same length.

The diagram in Figure 6-5 shows that the block size is 64 bits with DES. DES also uses a key to customize the encryption process, so that decryption can only be achieved by the person in possession of the same key that was used to encrypt. This is why this type of encryption is referred to as *symmetric encryption.*

The key is represented as 64 bits (8 bytes); however, only 56 of these are used by the algorithm. Eight bits are solely for error and parity checking which are then discarded; this means the effective key length is 56 bits.

As with other block-based encryption algorithms, DES by itself is not a secure system of encryption. DES must instead be used in different modes, which I discuss later in this chapter.

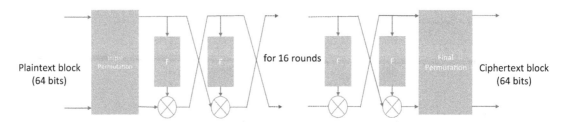

Figure 6-5. *The internal structure of DES*

The algorithm's overall structure is shown in the preceding diagram. There are 16 identical stages of processing which are called rounds. At the start of the process, there is an initial permutation. At the end of the encryption process, there is a final permutation. The initial permutation and final permutation have no cryptographic significance. They were included to make loading blocks in and out of mid-1970s 8-bit-based hardware more straightforward.

Before the main rounds, the block is divided into two 32-bit halves and processed alternately. This crisscrossing is known as the *Feistel scheme*, which is named after the German-born physicist and cryptographer Horst Feistel who performed pioneering research while working for IBM.

The Feistel structure is beneficial as the encryption, and decryption processes are similar which means they need only the key schedule to be reversed. This means that the size of the software required to implement such a cipher is nearly halved. The circle symbol with a cross in it, on the diagram, denotes the exclusive-OR (XOR) operation. The F-functions in the boxes scramble half of a block together with part of the encryption key.

The output from that function is then combined with the other half of the block. Then the halves are swapped before the next round in the process. After the final round is computed, the remaining halves are then swapped again; this is the feature of the Feistel structure that makes the encryption and decryption processes similar. DES uses a *key schedule* for encryption, which is an algorithm that generates the subkeys used for each of the 16 rounds.

First, the 56-bit key is divided into two 28-bit halves. Each half is then treated separately. In successive rounds, both halves are rotated left by one or two bits, and then 48 subkey bits are selected—24 bits from the left half and 24 from the right.

These rotations mean that a different set of bits is used in each subkey. The key schedule for decryption is similar, and the subkeys are in reverse order compared to encryption. Apart from that change, the process is the same as for encryption.

The encryption processes just described may seem complicated, but luckily, you do not need to know all of this in detail to use DES because the .NET implementation abstracts it away from you; but it is good to have an idea about how these algorithms work.

History of AES

The Advanced Encryption Standard (AES) is the latest encryption standard adopted by the National Institute of Standards and Technology (NIST) in 2001 for the symmetric encryption of messages. The AES algorithm was selected as part of a contest to find a replacement for DES. The AES algorithm is based on the Rijndael cipher that was developed by two Belgian cryptographers, Joan Daemen and Vincent Rijmen. Joan and Vincent submitted a proposal to NIST during the AES competition selection process. Rijndael is a family of ciphers that use different key and block sizes. For AES, NIST selected three different members of the Rijndael family. Each of these members has a block size of 128 bits, but three different key lengths: 128, 192, and 256 bits (see Figure 6-6).

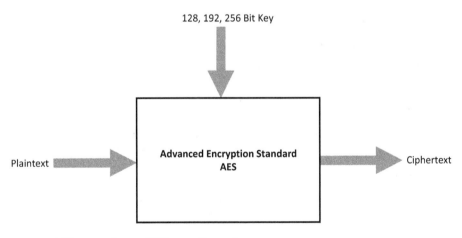

Figure 6-6. *AES uses three different key sizes*

AES is now used worldwide; it supersedes the DES. Like the DES algorithm, the AES algorithm is symmetric, which means that the same key is used for both encrypting and decrypting the data.

NIST announced that AES is the US standard FIPS 197 on November 26, 2001. This announcement followed a five-year standardization process in which 15 competing designs were presented and evaluated; the Rijndael cipher was selected as the most suitable. AES became active as a US government standard on May 26, 2002, after approval by the US Secretary of Commerce.

How AES Works

Unlike DES, AES does not use a Feistel network. AES is a variant of the Rijndael cipher that uses a fixed-block size of 128 bits and a variable sized key of 128, 192, or 256 bits. AES is based on a design principle that is known as a substitution-permutation network; this is a combination of both substitution and permutation and is fast in both software and hardware (see Figure 6-7).

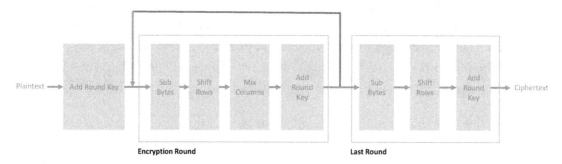

Figure 6-7. *The internal structure of AES*

A *substitution box*, or *S-box*, is a fundamental component of a symmetric key algorithm which performs substitutions. In a block cipher, the blocks obscure the relationship between the key and the resulting ciphertext. An S-box is implemented as a fixed lookup table.

A *permutation box*, or *P-box*, is a method of bit-shuffling to transpose bits across an S-boxes input. In block ciphers, the S-boxes and P-boxes make the relationship between plaintext and ciphertext challenging to understand.

One of the principal design goals of AES was to keep it more straightforward to implement in both hardware and software. AES works by repeating the same defined steps multiple times, which are called *rounds*. Each round of encryption comprises of several processing steps, including one that uses an encryption/decryption subkey that is generated from the shared key.

As mentioned, the proper key lengths in AES are 128, 192, and 256 bits. Every key is expanded so that a separate subkey could be utilized for every round. The number of AES rounds generally depends on the length of the key.

How Secure Is AES Against Brute-Force Attacks?

Current governments and enterprises place a lot of trust in the belief that AES is so secure that its security key can never be broken. The length of the key used in encryption determines the feasibility of performing a brute-force-based attack against it; longer keys are exponentially harder to crack than shorter keys.

A brute-force attack involves testing all possible key combinations of an encryption key until the correct key is discovered. Table 6-1 shows the potential number of key combinations for a given key size.

Table 6-1. *Total Combinations for Different Key Sizes*

Key Size	Possible Combinations
1-bit	2
2-bit	4
4-bit	16
8-bit	256
16-bit	65536
32-bit	4.2×10^9
56-bit (DES)	7.2×10^{16}
64-bit	1.8×10^{19}
128-bit (AES)	3.4×10^{38}
192-bit (AES)	6.2×10^{57}
256-bit (AES)	1.1×10^{77}

There is an exponential increase in combinations as the key size increases. From this table, you could argue that a 128-bit symmetric key is computationally secure against a brute-force attack.

Consider the times to crack in Table 6-1 compared to key sizes shown in Table 6-2.

Table 6-2. *Time to Brute Force Different Key Sizes*

Key Size	Time to Crack
56-bit	399 seconds
128-bit	1.02×10^{18} years
192-bit	1.872×10^{37} years
256-bit	3.31×10^{56} years

Even with a supercomputer at today's standards, it would take over 100 billion years to compromise a 128-bit AES key using a brute-force attack; this is much longer than the age of the universe, which is roughly 13.75 billion years old. If you assumed that a computational system existed somewhere that could brute force a DES key in about a second, it would still take that same machine roughly 149 trillion years to crack a 128-bit AES key.

Of course, we don't know what the future of computing holds in store, but for the moment, AES is a very secure algorithm that hasn't been compromised. Even though a 128-bit key should be more than sufficient, it is common to use a 256-bit key in practice.

This is what our code demo for AES will use.

API Commonality in the .NET Framework

We have looked at the history of each of the encryption algorithms, and we looked beneath the surface at how they work. Now, let's look at what the .NET Framework has to offer.

The AES, DES, and Triple DES algorithms in .NET all share a common abstract base class, `SymmetricAlgorithm`, which gives them a lot of standard functionality. Before we look at the specific algorithms and examples of their use, let's look at some of the characteristic properties associated with them.

Encryption Mode

The first property that we look at is the `Mode` property on the `SymmetricAlgorithm` object.

Block cipher algorithms such as AES, DES, and Triple DES encrypt data in block units rather than in single bytes at a time. Block ciphers use the same algorithm toward each block that is processed. Because of this, a block of plaintext always returns the same ciphertext when encrypted with the same key and algorithm.

Let's discuss the encryption modes.

- **Cipher block chaining (CBC)** mode introduces feedback into the encryption process. Before each plaintext block is encrypted, it is combined with the ciphertext of the previous block with a bitwise exclusive OR operation. This ensures that, even if the plaintext contains many identical blocks, they each encrypt to a different ciphertext block. The initialization vector (IV) is combined with the first plaintext block by a bitwise exclusive OR operation before the block is encrypted. We talk about the initialization vector in a moment.

- **Ciphertext feedback (CFB)** is an encryption mode that in contrast to the cipher block chaining, encrypts a specific number of bits at a time; it is at times desirable to encrypt and transfer some plaintext values instantly, one at a time. Like cipher block chaining, cipher feedback makes use of an initialization vector (IV). In cipher feedback mode, the previous ciphertext block is encrypted, and the output is XORed with the current plaintext block to create the current ciphertext block. The XOR operation conceals plaintext patterns. Plaintext cannot be directly worked on unless there is a retrieval of blocks from either the beginning or end of the ciphertext.

- **Ciphertext stealing (CTS)** handles any length of plaintext and produce ciphertext whose length is the same as the original plaintext length. This mode behaves like the CBC mode for all but the last two blocks of the plaintext.

- **Electronic codebook (ECB)** encrypts each block individually. Any blocks that are the same in any given message are translated into identical ciphertext blocks. The disadvantage of the electronic codebook mode is that identical plaintext blocks are encrypted to identical blocks and do not hide patterns of data very well. In some ways, it doesn't provide message confidentiality at all, and so it is not recommended for modern cryptographic protocols.

- **Output feedback (OFB)** processes small increments of plaintext data into ciphertext instead of treating an entire block at a time. This mode is similar to cipher feedback except it differs in the way the shift register is used. If a bit in your ciphertext changes, the corresponding bit of plaintext is replaced. However, if there are missing or extra bits of data from the ciphertext, the plaintext is mangled from that point on. The default mode in .NET for AES, DES, and Triple DES is cipher block chaining, and unless you have a reasonable need to change that default mode, you should go with the default.

Padding

The next property in SymmetricAlgorithm is padding, which specifies the padding to apply when the message block being encrypted is shorter than the total number of bytes needed for an encryption operation. There are different padding schemes, such as

- ANSI X923

- ISO 10126

- None

- PKCS7

- Zeros

The default padding in .NET for AES, DES, and Triple DES is the PKCS7 mode, and unless you have a good reason to change it, you should use the default.

Key

The Key property is a byte array that stores the encryption key prior to running encrypt and decrypt operations. The data in this property can literally be anything, but you should make sure you generate a secure key. There are two ways to do this. You can use the RNGCryptoServiceProvider object and generate a byte array to the desired key length, or you can call the GenerateKey() method. Under the covers the GenerateKey() method uses RNGCryptoServiceProvider to generate its key. Either way is fine. The examples used in this chapter all use the RNGCryptoServiceProvider object to generate the random number.

Initialization Vector (IV)

The initialization vector (IV) property is a byte array that stores a random number that is used along with the key for encryption. This number is also called a *nonce* (number once) and is employed only once in any encryption session. The use of an IV prevents repetition in data encryption, making it more difficult for a hacker who is using a dictionary attack to find patterns to break a cipher. For example, a sequence might appear twice or more within the body of a message.

If there are repeated sequences in encrypted data, an attacker could assume that the corresponding sequences in the plaintext message were the same. The initialization vector prevents the appearance of duplicated data sequences in the resulting ciphertext. Ideally, the initialization vector is a random number that is only known by the destination computer performing the decryption operation. The initialization vector can be agreed in advance of the encryption operation, transmitted independently, or included as part of the session that is set up before the exchange of the message data.

The length of the initialization vector (the number of bits or bytes it contains) depends on the method of encryption. The initialization vector does not have to be kept secret and can be transmitted or stored along with the message in the clear.

AesManaged and AesCryptoServiceProvider

The .NET Framework and .NET Core provide two implementations of the AES encryption algorithm, `AesManaged`, and `AesCryptoServiceProvider`. Which one should you use?

They both provide the same functionality in that they both implement the AES encryption specification, but the main difference is that `AesManaged` is a .NET-specific implementation, whereas `AesCryptoServiceProvider` uses the underlying cryptography libraries in Windows, macOS, or Linux, which are FIPS certified.

The National Institute of Standards and Technology (NIST) issued the FIPS 140-2 certification for cryptography modules that include both hardware and software. If you want to ensure you are encrypting data with AES by using a compliant implementation, then `AesCryptoServiceProvider` is the implementation that you want to use, especially if you need to interoperate with systems that are also compliant with FIPS 140-2. The code examples in the demo are based around `AesCryptoServiceProvider` and not `AesManaged`, although their usage is very similar.

Performing Symmetric Encryption with .NET

Now that we have spent time on symmetric encryption in .NET with DES, Triple DES, and AES, let's look at some example implementations. It is not a good idea to use DES or Triple DES in new software systems. If you are developing a new application, then you should use AES. If you work in an enterprise in which you have to integrate with older legacy systems that require you to encrypt or decrypt with DES or Triple DES, then understanding how to use them in .NET is a benefit for you. In the following code examples, I show you how to configure both the two- and three-key variations of Triple DES.

Before we look at a DES implementation, we first need to revisit our old friend the random-number generator quickly. The following code should look familiar to you because we used it in previous chapters. Here we need it to generate our symmetric encryption keys and initialization vectors.

```
public byte[] GenerateRandomNumber(int length)
{
    using (var randomNumberGenerator = new RNGCryptoServiceProvider())
    {
        var randomNumber = new byte[length];
        randomNumberGenerator.GetBytes(randomNumber);

        return randomNumber;
    }
}
```

In the GenerateRandomNumber method, we pass in an integer that represents the length of the byte array that we want to fill with random data. The random numbers are generated using the RNGCryptoServiceProvider object in the .NET Framework.

In the following code, a method encrypts data using DES.

```
public byte[] Encrypt(byte[] dataToEncrypt,
                      byte[] key,
                      byte[] iv)
{
    using (var des = new DESCryptoServiceProvider())
    {
```

```
    des.Mode = CipherMode.CBC;
    des.Padding = PaddingMode.PKCS7;

    des.Key = key;
    des.IV = iv;

    using (var memoryStream = new MemoryStream())
    {
        var cryptoStream =
            new CryptoStream(memoryStream,
            des.CreateEncryptor(),
            CryptoStreamMode.Write);

        cryptoStream.Write(dataToEncrypt, 0,
                        dataToEncrypt.Length);

        cryptoStream.FlushFinalBlock();

        return memoryStream.ToArray();
    }
  }
}
```

The Encrypt method takes three parameters, each of them byte arrays. The first
parameter is the data that we want to be encrypted. The next parameter is the encryption
key, and the final parameter is the initialization vector. The first thing that the Encrypt
method does is to create an instance of the DESCryptoServiceProvider object. Then
the padding and encryption modes are set explicitly. The values set in this example are
the default values, but I have set them to be explicit. Next, the key and the initialization
vectors are assigned that were passed in as parameters. I always like to generate them
myself and pass them in, but on the DESCryptoServiceProvider object, there are also
GenerateKey and GenerateIV methods that you can use instead if you so prefer.

Next, instances of MemoryStream and CryptoStream are created. The symmetric
encryption libraries in .NET are stream based, and the cryptography operations happen
within CryptoStream. As we are passing in the data to be encrypted into this method, we
can use a memory stream, but you could also use FileStream.

When we create the instance of the CryptoStream object, we pass in des.
CreateEncryptor(), which sets up the crypto stream with our configured
DESCryptoServiceProvider object.

```
var cryptoStream =
    new CryptoStream(memoryStream,
    des.CreateEncryptor(),
    CryptoStreamMode.Write);
```

Once the stream objects are set up, we then need to perform the actual encryption operation using the following code.

```
cryptoStream.Write(dataToEncrypt, 0, dataToEncrypt.Length);
cryptoStream.FlushFinalBlock();

return memoryStream.ToArray();
```

The call to Write takes the data we want to encrypt and its length in bytes and performs the encryption operation. Then we call FlushFinalBlock, which updates the data source with the current state of the buffer. Then the buffer is cleared. Our encrypted data is returned to the calling method.

Now that we have encrypted data, how do we decrypt it? The code for decrypting our data is almost identical to the method we just explored.

```
public byte[] Decrypt(byte[] dataToDecrypt,
                      byte[] key,
                      byte[] iv)
{
    using (var des = new DESCryptoServiceProvider())
    {
        des.Mode = CipherMode.CBC;
        des.Padding = PaddingMode.PKCS7;

        des.Key = key;
        des.IV = iv;

        using (var memoryStream = new MemoryStream())
        {
            var cryptoStream =
                new CryptoStream(memoryStream,
                des.CreateDecryptor(),
                CryptoStreamMode.Write);
```

```
        cryptoStream.Write(dataToDecrypt, 0,
                        dataToDecrypt.Length);

        cryptoStream.FlushFinalBlock();

        return memoryStream.ToArray();
      }
    }
}
```

At first glance, this code looks almost identical. Of course, the method name is different because we called Decrypt this time, and instead of passing in data to encrypt, we are passing in our encrypted data. The key and initialization vector should be the same as those used for the encryption process. If they are not the same, we will not be able to decrypt our data.

Apart from the method name and parameters, the only other difference in this method is the following lines of code.

```
var cryptoStream =
        new CryptoStream(memoryStream,
        des.CreateDecryptor(),
        CryptoStreamMode.Write);

        cryptoStream.Write(dataToDecrypt, 0,
            dataToDecrypt.Length);
```

When we create the CryptoStream, instead of passing in the CreateEncryptor method on the DESCryptoServiceProvider instance, we pass in CreateDecryptor instead, also on the call to Write on the CryptoStream, we pass in the encrypted data that we want to be decrypted. These are the only differences between the code for encrypting and decrypting with DES. The code for performing Triple DES and AES is also very similar.

Let's now look at a simple console application that calls into this encryption and decryption for DES.

```
class Program
{
    static void Main(string[] args)
    {
        var des = new DesEncryption();
        var key = des.GenerateRandomNumber(8);
        var iv = des.GenerateRandomNumber(8);
        const string original = "Text to encrypt";

        var encrypted = des.Encrypt(
                    Encoding.UTF8.GetBytes(original),
                    key, iv);

        var decrypted = des.Decrypt(encrypted, key, iv);

        var decryptedMessage =
                    Encoding.UTF8.GetString(decrypted);

        Console.WriteLine("DES Demonstration in .NET");
        Console.WriteLine("-------------------------");
        Console.WriteLine();
        Console.WriteLine("Original Text = " + original);

        Console.WriteLine("Encrypted Text = "
                    + Convert.ToBase64String(encrypted));

        Console.WriteLine("Decrypted Text = "
                    + decryptedMessage);

        Console.ReadLine();
    }
}
```

The demo application starts by creating an instance of a class containing our encryption and decryption methods. Then we create the key and initialization vector. The key we generate is 8 bytes (64 bits). The actual DES key that is used is 56 bits, so our key is padded for the extra bits. The initialization vector is also 8 bits in length.

Next, the code performs our actual encryption and decryption operations.

```
var encrypted = des.Encrypt(
        Encoding.UTF8.GetBytes(original),
        key, iv);

var decrypted = des.Decrypt(encrypted, key, iv);

var decryptedMessage =
        Encoding.UTF8.GetString(decrypted);
```

When we call the Encrypt operation, we first have to convert the string we want to encrypt into a byte array. In this case, we are using UTF8.GetBytes to perform this conversion. When the Encrypt method returns, it passes back a byte array containing the encrypted data, which means that when we call decrypt, we do not have to perform any conversions because the data to decrypt is already a byte array.

When the Decrypt operation returns it passes back the unencrypted data, but it is also in byte array form, so if we want to display it to the user in its original form, we first have to convert it to a string using UTF8.GetString. When we run the demo, we end up with something like you see in Figure 6-8.

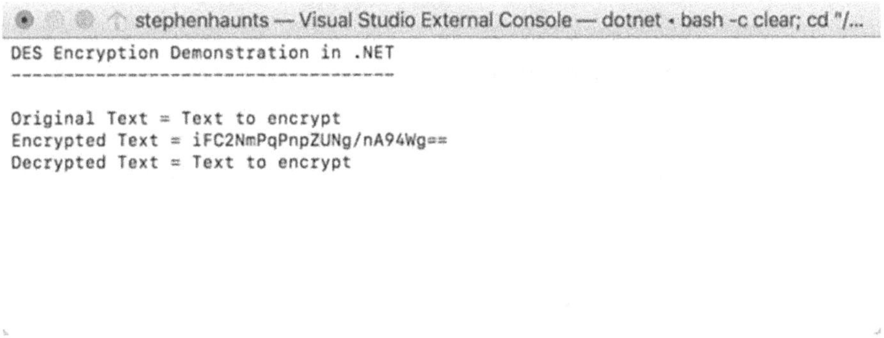

Figure 6-8. *The result of DES encryption*

Now that we have looked at how to use DES in .NET, let's expand on it to use Triple DES. The only changes to our original encrypt and decrypt methods are the name of the CryptoServiceProvider class that we instantiate. In the demo we just looked at, it was DESCryptoServiceProvider, but in the next demo, it is TripleDESCryptoServiceProvider. This means our Encrypt method looks like the following.

```
public byte[] Encrypt(byte[] dataToEncrypt,
                      byte[] key, byte[] iv)
{
    using (var des = new TripleDESCryptoServiceProvider())
    {
        des.Mode = CipherMode.CBC;
        des.Padding = PaddingMode.PKCS7;

        des.Key = key;
        des.IV = iv;

        using (var memoryStream = new MemoryStream())
        {
            var cryptoStream =
                new CryptoStream(memoryStream,
                des.CreateEncryptor(),
                CryptoStreamMode.Write);

            cryptoStream.Write(dataToEncrypt, 0,
                dataToEncrypt.Length);

            cryptoStream.FlushFinalBlock();

            return memoryStream.ToArray();
        }
    }
}
```

As you can see, the only work that has changed in the Encrypt method is the class name TripleDESCryptoServiceProvider. The same is also true for the Decrypt method. The only change is the change from DESCryptoServiceProvider to TripleDESCryptoServiceProvider, so there is no need to repeat it here.

What is different though is how we handle the keys that we pass into Encrypt and Decrypt. We discussed earlier that you could use Triple DES in two configurations. The first uses two encryption keys and the second uses three encryption keys.

The following is an example sample application that uses our encryption code.

```
class Program
{
    static void Main(string[] args)
    {
        var tripleDes = new TripleDesEncryption();

        var key = tripleDes.GenerateRandomNumber(16);

        var iv = tripleDes.GenerateRandomNumber(8);
        const string original = "Text to encrypt";

        var encrypted = tripleDes.Encrypt(
                Encoding.UTF8.GetBytes(original), key, iv);

        var decrypted = tripleDes.Decrypt(encrypted, key, iv);

        var decryptedMessage =
                Encoding.UTF8.GetString(decrypted);

        Console.WriteLine("Triple DES Demonstration in .NET");
        Console.WriteLine("--------------------------------");
        Console.WriteLine();
        Console.WriteLine("Original Text = " + original);
        Console.WriteLine("Encrypted Text = " +
                        Convert.ToBase64String(encrypted));

        Console.WriteLine("Decrypted Text = " + decryptedMessage);
    }
}
```

This code is very similar to the code we used to test DES, but in this example, there is one main difference in the size of the encryption key that we are generating.

```
var key = tripleDes.GenerateRandomNumber(16);
```

Instead of generating a single 8-byte key, of with 56 bits are used, and the rest is padding, we are creating 16 bytes; this means the .NET of Triple DES operate in the two-key variation. If we want to use the three-key variation, then we generate a key that is 24 bytes long by calling the following code.

```
var key = tripleDes.GenerateRandomNumber(24);
```

Now that we have explored DES and Triple DES in some detail, what about the AES?

```
public byte[] Encrypt(byte[] dataToEncrypt,
                      byte[] key,
                      byte[] iv)
{
    using (var aes = new AesCryptoServiceProvider())
    {
        aes.Mode = CipherMode.CBC;
        aes.Padding = PaddingMode.PKCS7;

        aes.Key = key;
        aes.IV = iv;

        using (var memoryStream = new MemoryStream())
        {
            var cryptoStream = new CryptoStream(
                memoryStream,
                aes.CreateEncryptor(),
                CryptoStreamMode.Write);

            cryptoStream.Write(dataToEncrypt, 0,
                            dataToEncrypt.Length);

            cryptoStream.FlushFinalBlock();

            return memoryStream.ToArray();
        }
    }
}
```

Luckily, the code to use AES in .NET is almost identical to what we just looked at for DES and Triple DES. As you can see in the preceding example code, the only change to the code is the service provider class that we instantiate; this time it is AesCryptoServiceProvider, everything else is the same.

```
static void Main(string[] args)
{
    var aes = new AesEncryption();
    var key = aes.GenerateRandomNumber(32);
    var iv = aes.GenerateRandomNumber(16);
    const string original = "Text to encrypt";

    var encrypted = aes.Encrypt(
                    Encoding.UTF8.GetBytes(original), key, iv);

    var decrypted = aes.Decrypt(encrypted, key, iv);
    var decryptedMessage = Encoding.UTF8.GetString(decrypted);

    Console.WriteLine("AES Encryption in .NET");
    Console.WriteLine("----------------------");
    Console.WriteLine();
    Console.WriteLine("Original Text = " + original);
    Console.WriteLine("Encrypted Text = " +
                    Convert.ToBase64String(encrypted));
    Console.WriteLine("Decrypted Text = " + decryptedMessage);

    Console.ReadLine();
}
```

With the AES code almost identical to the DES and Triple DES, the only difference in the usage of the AES encryption and decryption code are the key sizes and the size of the initialization vector. The initialization vector is 16 bytes. For the key sizes, we have three different options: 128 bits, 192 bits, and 256 bits. This means the byte arrays are 16 bytes, 24 bytes, and 32 bytes, respectively. The preceding code sample uses 32 bytes or 256 bits for the key that has the most robust size. I would say that unless you have a specific reason to use a small key size, go straight for the 256-bit (32 bytes) key. The result of our AES sample application is seen in Figure 6-9.

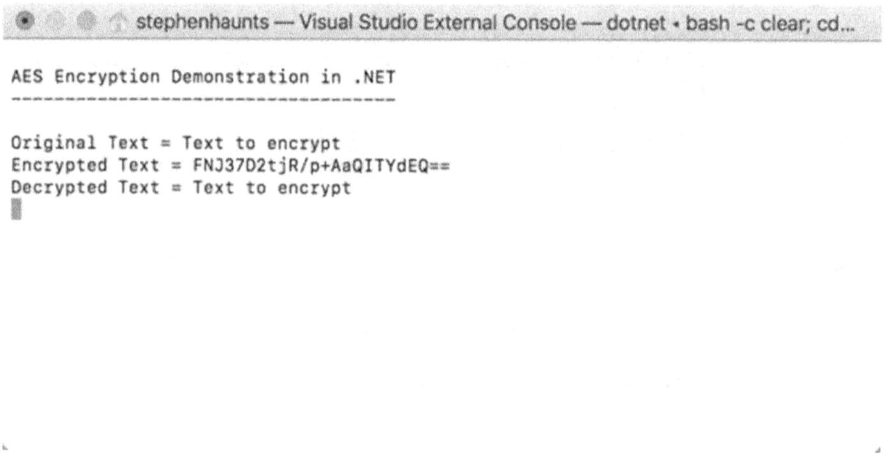

```
⦿  ⦿  ⌂  stephenhaunts — Visual Studio External Console — dotnet • bash -c clear; cd...

AES Encryption Demonstration in .NET
-----------------------------------------

Original Text = Text to encrypt
Encrypted Text = FNJ37D2tjR/p+AaQITYdEQ==
Decrypted Text = Text to encrypt
```

Figure 6-9. *The result of AES encryption*

Summary

In this chapter, we started exploring the confidentiality pillar in our pursuit of using cryptography. Our primary focus was to look at symmetric encryption. Symmetric encryption is where you use the same key to both encrypt and decrypt data. Symmetric encryption is fast and efficient due to its algorithmic nature, but it does have one major downside in that sharing the encryption key between parties is hard to do securely, which is something we explore later in the book.

We started by looking at DES and its more secure variant, Triple DES. Although DES and Triple DES are not recommended in new software solutions, they are worth talking about because there are many legacy systems that use a variant of DES internally, so you may be in a situation where you need to encrypt or decrypt data with DES.

AES is preferable encryption algorithm to use in .NET. AES is a modern and secure encryption algorithm that allows you to use key sizes of 128 bits, 193 bits, or 256 bits.

All three encryption algorithms inherit from the `SymmetricAlgorithm` base class, which means they are all identical to use which is excellent for programmer usability. The main differences are in the key sizes utilized and the sizes of the initialization vectors.

In the next chapter, we continue our exploration of the confidentiality pillar by looking at asymmetric cryptography.

CHAPTER 7

Asymmetric Encryption

In Chapter 6, we looked at symmetric encryption, which is a two-way encryption process that uses the same key for both encryption and decryption of your message, as shown in Figure 7-1. In the diagram, we have plaintext, or our original data, represented on the left, which is then encrypted with a key to produce our encrypted data, or ciphertext. That data is decrypted using the same key to uncover the original data, or plaintext. This process is referred to as *symmetric encryption* because we use the same key for both encryption and decryption.

Figure 7-1. *Symmetric encryption*

In Chapter 6, we looked at some advantages and disadvantages of symmetric encryption.

Advantage: Very Secure

When using a secure algorithm such as AES, symmetric encryption is exceptionally secure. One of the most widely used, symmetric, key encryption systems is the US government-designated AES. As of the writing of this book, AES is unbroken, so it is one of the recommended algorithms.

© Stephen Haunts 2019
S. Haunts, *Applied Cryptography in .NET and Azure Key Vault*,
https://doi.org/10.1007/978-1-4842-4375-6_7

Advantage: Fast

One of the problems with public key encryption systems like RSA is that they need complicated mathematics to work, which makes them computationally intensive and slow. Encrypting and decrypting symmetric key data is easier, which gives you excellent read and write performance. In fact, many solid-state drives, which are very fast, use symmetric key encryption store data, yet they are still a lot faster than unencrypted standard hard drives.

Disadvantage: Sharing Keys Is Hard

One of the most significant problems with symmetric key encryption algorithms is that you need to have a way to get the key to the person with whom you are sending the encrypted data. Encryption keys aren't simple strings of text like passwords; they are byte arrays of randomly generated data, such as the random numbers we created with `RNGCryptoServiceProvider` earlier in the book. As such, you need to have a safe way to get the key to the other person.

With this in mind, symmetric key encryption is particularly useful when encrypting your information as opposed to when sharing encrypted information. There are ways to use the power of symmetric encryption with a suitable key sharing scheme, which we explore in another chapter when I talk about hybrid encryption schemes.

Disadvantage: Dangerous If Compromised

When someone gets hold of one of your symmetric keys, they can decrypt everything encrypted with that key. When you're using symmetric encryption for two-way communications, this means that both sides of the conversation get compromised. With asymmetric cryptography, such as RSA, if someone gets your private key, they can decrypt messages sent to you, but they can't decrypt what you sent to the other recipient because it was encrypted with a completely different key pair.

With this in mind, let's take a closer look at asymmetric encryption.

What Is Asymmetric Encryption?

The main problem with symmetric encryption is that of securely sharing keys. For a recipient to decrypt a message, they need the same key as the sender, and this exchange of keys can be difficult to do securely. An excellent solution to this problem is to use asymmetric cryptography, which is also referred to as *public key cryptography*.

With public key cryptography, you have two keys. A *public key*, which anyone can know, and a *private key*, which only the recipient of a message knows. These keys are mathematically linked. The message sender uses the public key to encrypt a message, and the recipient uses their private key to decrypt the message; this is demonstrated in Figure 7-2.

The word *asymmetric* is used because this method uses two different linked keys that perform inverse operations, whereas symmetric cryptography uses the same key to perform both operations.

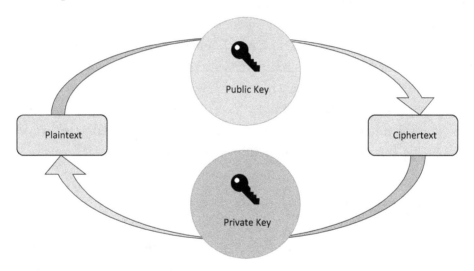

***Figure 7-2.** Asymmetric encryption*

It is quite straightforward to generate both the public and private key pair, but the power of asymmetric cryptography comes from the fact it is impossible for a private key to be determined from its corresponding public key. It is only the private key that needs to be kept secret in the key pair.

The primary advantage to using asymmetric encryption is that two parties don't need to have pre-shared a secret key to communicate using asymmetric encryption. The person encrypting a message only needs to know the recipient's public key, which is available to anyone on request. Then only the recipient can decrypt the message with their private key. The main disadvantage is that the asymmetric algorithm is comparatively complex when compared to symmetric encryption, which means that messages take longer to encrypt and decrypt.

The History of RSA

RSA is a public key encryption technology developed by RSA Security LLC (formerly RSA Security, Inc.). The name RSA forms an acronym that stands for the names of its creators, Rivest, Shamir, and Adelman. RSA gets its power from the idea that there is no efficient way to factor huge prime numbers. Deducing an RSA key requires an extraordinary amount of computer processing power and time. The RSA algorithm has become the de facto standard for industrial-strength encryption, especially for data sent over the Internet. RSA is built into many software products.

There is a drawback to RSA, though. You can only encrypt data that is smaller than the size of the key, which makes RSA quite limited. It is more common to use RSA to encrypt a randomly generated, symmetric AES key, which means you can send the RSA-encrypted AES key safely to a recipient and then use AES with that key to encrypt your data.

We explore this option in the next module on hybrid encryption. You could, of course, split your data into smaller chunks and encrypt each of these in turn, and then when you decrypt your data chunks, combine the results back together to form your original message, but this would be incredibly inefficient with RSA.

How Does RSA Work?

RSA typically uses three key sizes: 1024 bit, 2048 bit, and 4096 bit. By today's standards, you should use at least a 2048-bit key because 1024-bit keys are now considered weak. Ideally, use the largest key size, 4096 bits, but 2048 bits is acceptable.

Key Derivation

The public and private key pairs in RSA are based on prime numbers, and their security comes from the difficulty in factorizing prime numbers. What this means is that if you have a large prime number, it is tough to determine what two prime numbers are multiplied together to make the larger number.

Let's look at a simple example.

If you were to pick two prime numbers, let's say 23 and 17, and I asked you to multiply these numbers, you could work it out quite comfortably in your head or with a calculator. The answer is 391. But if I were to ask you which two prime numbers do you multiply to make 5963, it would be a harder mathematical problem to solve. The answer is $67 \times 89 = 5963$.

Now imagine numbers that are considerably larger, for example, a 2048-bit number or 256-byte number. The strength of RSA keys is because going from one large number back to the original primes that made that number initially is a tough problem to solve, which is where the strength of RSA comes into effect.

Now let's equate this example back to private and public keys. Alice wishes to send an important message to Bob, so she uses Bob's public key to encrypt the message. In the simple example we just looked at, the public key is 5963. Alice then encrypts the message and sends it to Bob, where he uses his private key to decrypt the message. In our example, the private key consists of the two prime numbers: 67 and 89.

This is a very simplified example. The reality is more complicated and goes outside the scope of this book because there are many more components to an RSA key than just the prime numbers, but it is beneficial for you to have this simplified mental model of an RSA key.

In Figure 7-3, the internals of a public and private key in .NET are shown in the debugger. The class we use to hold an RSA key is called `RSAParameters`.

Watch 1			▾ ⊡ ×
Name	Value	Type	
▲ 🔧 publicKey	{System.Security.Cryptography.RSAParameters}	System.Security.Cryptography.RSAParameters	
D	null	byte[]	
DP	null	byte[]	
DQ	null	byte[]	
▷ Exponent	{byte[3]}	byte[]	
InverseQ	null	byte[]	
▷ Modulus	{byte[256]}	byte[]	
P	null	byte[]	
Q	null	byte[]	
▲ 🔧 privateKey	{System.Security.Cryptography.RSAParameters}	System.Security.Cryptography.RSAParameters	
▷ D	{byte[256]}	byte[]	
▷ DP	{byte[128]}	byte[]	
▷ DQ	{byte[128]}	byte[]	
▷ Exponent	{byte[3]}	byte[]	
▷ InverseQ	{byte[128]}	byte[]	
▷ Modulus	{byte[256]}	byte[]	
▷ P	{byte[128]}	byte[]	
▷ Q	{byte[128]}	byte[]	

***Figure 7-3.** Observing RSA keys in the debugger*

As you can see in the screenshot, there are more components to the public and private key.

- **P** is one of our prime numbers.

- **Q** is the other prime number.

- **Modulus** is the result of both prime numbers multiplied together as demonstrated a moment ago.

- **Exponent** is called the public exponent.

- **InverseQ** is the inverse Q coefficient.

- **D** is the private exponent that is only present in the private key.

- **DP** and **DQ** are exponents that are only present in the private key.

The relevant parts to note are that in the private key, P and Q are both populated; they are the two prime numbers. In the public key, P and Q are not present because they are secret to anyone who uses the public key; but the modulus is populated, which is the result of multiplying the two prime numbers.

Encryption and Decryption

Unlike symmetric encryption algorithms such as AES, where the encryption and decryption process are algorithmic (the plaintext is split it into smaller blocks and run through several rounds of obfuscation with the key), RSA takes a more mathematical approach and is based on modular arithmetic.

In mathematics, modular arithmetic is an integer-based system, where numbers "wrap around" when reaching a certain value. This wrap around value is called the modulus. A favorite example for describing the use of modular arithmetic is defining a 12-hour clock, where a 24-hour day is divided into two 12-hour blocks.

If the time is 7:00 a.m., then it will be 3:00 p.m. eight hours later.

A standard addition would suggest that the time should be 15.00 (7 + 8 = 15), but because we are dealing with a day that is split into two 12-hour blocks, it is not the correct answer because the clock will wrap around every 12 hours.

As another example, if we have the clock set to at 12:00 (noon) and 21 hours pass, then the correct time will be 9:00 a.m. the next day, rather than 33:00; this is because the hour number will start over again once it reaches 12; this is referred to as arithmetic modulo 12.

Because the encryption process is mathematical and based on Modulus arithmetic, there are limits to the amount of data you can encrypt in one go. As a rule, you cannot encrypt data larger than the size of the key. So, if you are encrypting using a 2048-bit key, which is 256 bytes in length, then you cannot encrypt more than 256 bytes. The more data you encrypt, the slower the encryption process is even though RSA makes the key sharing problem easier, it is quite an inefficient encryption system.

RSA in .NET

As with the symmetric encryption implementation in .NET, the application of RSA is straightforward; if anything, it is easier, which is excellent news. The main class that you need is RSACryptoServiceProvider, which is used for key generation as well as encryption and decryption.

Let's look at key generation first.

In-Memory Keys

You generate RSA key pairs by first constructing the RSACryptoServiceProvider class.

```
private RSAParameters _publicKey;
private RSAParameters _privateKey;

public void AssignNewKey()
{
    using (var rsa = new RSACryptoServiceProvider(2048))
    {
        rsa.PersistKeyInCsp = false;
        _publicKey = rsa.ExportParameters(false);
        _privateKey = rsa.ExportParameters(true);
    }
}
```

Valid lengths for the key size parameter that you pass into the constructor are 1024 bits, 2048 bits, and 4096 bits. In the preceding example code, we are creating a public and a private key and keeping them in objects in memory. We look at what the PersistKeyInCsp property means in a moment, but for this example, it is set to false. To export the key material, you call the ExportParameters method on the RSA object instance of RSACryptoServiceProvider. To export the public key, you pass false into ExportParameters; to export the private key, you pass in true.

If you are using .NET Core, then this method of creating keys using RSACryptoServiceProvider works cross-platform across Windows, macOS, and Linux, which is the only supported way of creating the RSA keys programmatically across all three platforms. The next two techniques for XML keys and CSP keys only work on Windows.

XML-Based Keys

The next method of key generation supported by RSACryptoServiceProvider is to export or import XML-based keys. In the following code example, we pass in two parameters, which represent the file names of the public and private keys that you want to generate. Next, we create an instance of RSACryptoServiceProvider and pass in our key length. In this example, we are using a 2048-bit key. Again, we are setting the PersistKeyInCsp flag to false again.

```
public void AssignNewKey(string publicKeyPath,
                         string privateKeyPath)
{
    using (var rsa = new RSACryptoServiceProvider(2048))
    {
        rsa.PersistKeyInCsp = false;

        File.WriteAllText(publicKeyPath,
            rsa.ToXmlString(false));

        File.WriteAllText(privateKeyPath,
            rsa.ToXmlString(true));
    }
}
```

Next, in this example, we use the WriteAllText static method on the File class to save out the XML text of the public and private keys to disk. To export the actual key material, we use the ToXmlString method on the RSACryptoServiceParameter instance.

It is important to stress though, that just because you can export RSA keys as XML files, you should question your need to do this. If you need to do this for development tools or other tooling, then that's fine. If you intend to export RSA keys and store them in a folder on a server somewhere for a production system, then this is not a good idea at all. Files are tough to protect. Your servers are susceptible to being accessed by people who shouldn't, and they could copy, delete, or tamper with keys. There are much better ways to use keys: use the cryptographic service provider (Windows only), load keys from the certificate store (also Windows only), or use a protected key vault, such as Azure Key Vault, which is covered later in the book.

Cryptographic Service Provider

Storing private keys on the file system is not a great idea, but if you are using a Windows-based system, then you can use Windows inbuilt key container system called the *cryptographic service provider* (CSP). A key container in Windows is a place that the operating system can store keys, and they can be stored at the user level or the machine level. The machine-level key containers are available to all users, and the user level containers are only available to the user that created or imported that key container. The following code generates a set of keys and stores them in a named container.

```
const string ContainerName = "MyContainer";

public void AssignNewKey()
{
    CspParameters cspParams = new CspParameters(1)
    {
        KeyContainerName = ContainerName,
        Flags = CspProviderFlags.UseMachineKeyStore,
        ProviderName =
                "Microsoft Strong Cryptographic Provider"
    };

    var rsa = new RSACryptoServiceProvider(cspParams)
    {
        PersistKeyInCsp = true
    };
}
```

To generate an RSA asymmetric key and store it within a key container you need first to instantiate the CspParameters class and pass in the name that you want to call the key container to the CspParameters.KeyContainerName field. Using the Flags property, you have a choice of storing the key in either a local user key container or a machine-level key container.

In our example, we are using a machine-level key store. The `ProviderName` field represents a specific name used for a key container on the system. The default Windows provider is the Microsoft Strong Cryptographic Provider. If you are using any specific key management hardware that is compatible with the Windows CSP, then the name you provide in that string relates to the hardware whose drivers should be installed on the system.

Key containers that are at the user level are stored inside the Windows user profile for that user. The key container can then be used to encrypt and decrypt data for any applications that run using that user identity. Having key containers at the user level is useful if you require that the RSA keys are removed with the user profile is deleted. However, because you must be logged in with the specific user account that makes use of the user-level RSA key container to encrypt or decrypt protected configuration sections, they are inconvenient to use.

In addition to the user-level RSA key containers, there are machine-level containers that can be available to every user that logs into a computer. Machine-level key containers are useful because you can use them to both encrypt and decrypt data while logged in with any user account, including admin accounts. Although machine-level RSA key containers are available to all users, they can be secured with NTFS access control lists (ACLs) so that only required users can access them.

Next, you create a new instance of the `RSACryptoServiceProvider` and pass the previously created `CspParameters` object to its constructor.

```
var rsa = new RSACryptoServiceProvider(cspParams)
{
    PersistKeyInCsp = true
};
```

When you provide a `CspParameters` object to the `RSACryptoServiceProvider`, the `PersistKeyInCsp` flag is automatically set to true, but in this example, I have set it explicitly for illustrative purposes.

```
public void DeleteKeyInCsp()
{
    var cspParams = new CspParameters
    {
        KeyContainerName = ContainerName
    };
```

```
var rsa = new RSACryptoServiceProvider(cspParams)
{
    PersistKeyInCsp = false
};

rsa.Clear();
}
```

To remove a key from a key container, you first need to instantiate another instance of the CspParameters class and pass the name of the key container to the CspParameters.KeyContainerName property. Then you create a new instance of a class RSACryptoServiceProvider and pass the previously created CspParameters object to its constructor. Next, set the PersistKeyInCSP property of the RSACryptoServiceProvider class to false. Finally, you need to call the Clear method on the instance of RSACryptoServiceProvider. Calling this method releases all resources of the RSA instance and clears the key container.

Encryption and Decryption

Now that we have looked at generating RSA public and private keys, let's take a look at the encryption and decryption process. Our first example is based on having your public and private keys loaded into local RSAParameters properties, as shown in the following code.

```
private RSAParameters _publicKey;
private RSAParameters _privateKey;

public byte[] EncryptData(byte[] dataToEncrypt)
{
    byte[] cipherbytes;

    using (var rsa = new RSACryptoServiceProvider())
    {
        rsa.PersistKeyInCsp = false;
        rsa.ImportParameters(_publicKey);

        cipherbytes = rsa.Encrypt(dataToEncrypt, true);
    }

    return cipherbytes;
}
```

Once you have your keys set up, the encryption process is very straightforward. If you look at the code snippet, you pass in your data to encrypt as a byte array and then create a new instance of RSACryptoServiceProvider. You import the public key to encrypt with using the ImportParamters method, and you have to make sure PersistKeyInCSP is set to false. Then you call the Encrypt method on the RSACryptoServiceProvider object.

The second parameter on the encrypt method is for *optimal asymmetric encryption padding* (OEAP), which is a padding scheme that is used within RSA. OEAP is a form of the Feistel network that is designed to add an element of randomness to the encryption process, which helps prevent the partial decryption of ciphertext by ensuring that an attacker cannot recover any portion of the plaintext.

Once you have called Encrypt, you get a byte array back containing your encrypted data. The encryption process is similar if you are using a key container.

Let's now look at the decryption process as shown in the following code.

```
public byte[] DecryptData(byte[] dataToEncrypt)
{
    byte[] plain;

    using (var rsa = new RSACryptoServiceProvider())
    {
        rsa.PersistKeyInCsp = false;

        rsa.ImportParameters(_privateKey);
        plain = rsa.Decrypt(dataToEncrypt, true);
    }

    return plain;
}
```

The code looks virtually identical to the Encrypt method, apart from where we load the private key instead of the public key, and we call Decrypt instead of Encrypt. Remember that with RSA, we encrypt using our recipient's public key, which they are free to share with us, and they decrypt the message using their private key, which only they know.

If we were to write a method to call this encryption and decryption process, it might look something like the following.

```
private static void RsaWithRsaParameterKey()
{
    var rsaParams = new RSAWithRSAParameterKey();
```

```
const string original = "Text to encrypt";

rsaParams.AssignNewKey();

var encrypted =
    rsaParams.EncryptData(
        Encoding.UTF8.GetBytes(original));

var decrypted =
    rsaParams.DecryptData(encrypted);

Console.WriteLine("RSA Encryption Demonstration in .NET");
Console.WriteLine("-----------------------------------");
Console.WriteLine();
Console.WriteLine("In Memory Key");
Console.WriteLine();
Console.WriteLine("   Original Text = " + original);
Console.WriteLine("   Encrypted Text = "
    + Convert.ToBase64String(encrypted));

Console.WriteLine("   Decrypted Text = "
    + Encoding.Default.GetString(decrypted));
}
```

First, we create an instance of our class that contains the Encrypt and Decrypt methods. Then we call the code to assign a new key. In this example, the public and private keys are stored as members' variables. Then we call the Encrypt method, but first, our data to encrypt, which is a string, is first converted into a byte array using Encoding.UTF8.GetBytes. Once the Encrypt method returns, we have our encrypted data (which used the public key for encryption) as a byte array.

Then the example code decrypts the data by passing in the encrypted byte array to Decrypt. This time the decryption happens using the private key to recover the plaintext, which is also sent back as a byte array. Then the sample code prints the original message, converts the encrypted ciphertext into a base64 string for display, and turns the decrypted plaintext back into a string. You can see the results of this in the screenshot in Figure 7-4.

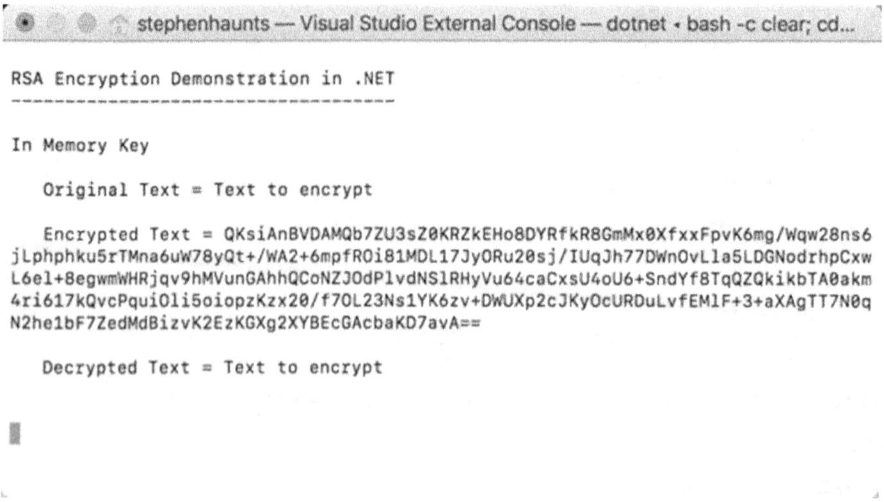

Figure 7-4. *Example result of encrypting some text with RSA*

Encrypted and decrypting with XML-based keys is very similar, except there is one small difference, as shown in the following code.

```
public byte[] EncryptData(string publicKeyPath,
                          byte[] dataToEncrypt)
{
    byte[] cipherbytes;

    using (var rsa = new RSACryptoServiceProvider(2048))
    {
        rsa.PersistKeyInCsp = false;
        rsa.FromXmlString(File.ReadAllText(publicKeyPath));

        cipherbytes = rsa.Encrypt(dataToEncrypt, false);
    }

    return cipherbytes;
}

public byte[] DecryptData(string privateKeyPath,
                          byte[] dataToEncrypt)
{
    byte[] plain;
```

```
    using (var rsa = new RSACryptoServiceProvider(2048))
    {
        rsa.PersistKeyInCsp = false;
        rsa.FromXmlString(File.ReadAllText(privateKeyPath));
        plain = rsa.Decrypt(dataToEncrypt, false);
    }

    return plain;
}
```

When encrypting and decrypting, instead of calling ImportParameters to load the keys, we call FromXmlString and pass in the results of loading the key from disk. Again, loading keys from disk like this is very risky, and I don't recommend storing RSA keys as files, but you can do it if needed. Remember that using XML-based keys only works on the Windows version of .NET Framework and .NET Core. This operation is not supported on macOS and Linux as of .NET Core 2.1.

What if you are using the CSP key container? The code is very similar, but there is a small change to load the keys from the key container.

```
public byte[] EncryptData(byte[] dataToEncrypt)
{
    byte[] cipherbytes;

    var cspParams = new CspParameters
    {
        KeyContainerName = ContainerName
    };

  using (var rsa = new RSACryptoServiceProvider(2048,
            cspParams))
    {
        cipherbytes = rsa.Encrypt(dataToEncrypt, false);
    }

    return cipherbytes;
}

public byte[] DecryptData(byte[] dataToDecrypt)
{
    byte[] plain;
```

```
var cspParams = new CspParameters
{
    KeyContainerName = ContainerName
};
using (var rsa = new RSACryptoServiceProvider(2048,
    cspParams))
{
    plain = rsa.Decrypt(dataToDecrypt, false);
}

return plain;
}
```

In both the Encrypt and Decrypt methods, we construct a new CspParameters object and load in the container name into the KeyContainerName property. Then when we construct the RSSCryptoServiceProvider class, we pass in the CspParameters instance as the seconds' constructor parameter, which loads the relevant key, and there is no need to import or load the keys manually.

Summary

In this chapter, we covered the second part of our confidentiality pillar of cryptography. Asymmetric encryption involves using an algorithm like RSA that uses split public and private keys to encrypt data. By using split keys like this, we overcome the problem we discussed with symmetric encryption where the key is hard to share between a sender and receiver of a message. With asymmetric encryption, this isn't an issue. The recipient of a message has two keys, a public, and a private key. The public key they can share with anyone, and the private key they keep secret. If you wanted to send a message to the recipient, you get their public key, and encrypt your message and send it to them. They then use their private key to recover the message.

If they want to send you a reply, they get your public key and encrypt their message, which they then send you, and you use your private key to recover the message. Using split public and private keys like this means that you need two sets of public and private key pairs for a two-way conversation, one for each receiver.

In the next chapter, we look at the final cryptographic pillar: non-repudiation.

CHAPTER 8

Digital Signatures

So far, we have covered three pillars of our four pillars of cryptography. We discussed integrity and how cryptographic primitives, like hashing with SHA-256, can help us solve that problem. We then discussed authentication and I explained hashed message authentication codes, such as HMAC-SHA-256. A HMAC is similar to a standard hashing function, but it differs in that you have to provide a key to the hashing function which means for anyone to calculate the same hash code for a piece of data, they also need to be in possession of that key, this is why it is authenticated.

We then covered confidentiality by looking at both symmetric and asymmetric encryption. For symmetric encryption, we used primitives like DES, Triple DES, and the Advanced Encryption Standard (AES), where you use the same key for both encryption and decryption. For new systems, I recommend going straight to AES with at least a 256-bit (32 bytes) key. You may still encounter DES and Triple DES if you have to work with older legacy systems, but I don't recommend using DES or Triple DES for new systems. For asymmetric cryptography, we looked at RSA which uses a split public and private key system for managing encryption. You use your recipient's public key for encryption, and then the recipient uses their private key to decrypt the data.

The final pillar we want to look at is non-repudiation. An essential function of cryptography is to ensure non-repudiation of a sent message, which is where the receiver of the message cannot deny that the message is authentic. A digital signature is a technique used to help demonstrate this authenticity of the message. A digital signature gives the recipient of the signature the reason to believe that an identified sender created the original message, this is important because it means that the sender cannot deny sending the message in the first place.

Before I go into detail about digital signatures, let's look at an example from the physical world that works as an analog to digital signatures. Let's say you are a contractor/consultant, and you are singing a contract for some work that pays $30,000 on completion. When you sign the contract with the company, you sign it, the company director signs it and they have a representative from human resources sign it too as a witness.

© Stephen Haunts 2019
S. Haunts, *Applied Cryptography in .NET and Azure Key Vault*,
https://doi.org/10.1007/978-1-4842-4375-6_8

You go and do the work, and once it is completed, you invoice the company but instead invoice for $40,000. The company can turn around and easily say that, no, you signed a contract for $30,000, and prove it with the signature of the director and the witness from human resources, so if it ever went to a legal battle, they have that signed contract to refer too; this is non-repudiation at work in the real world. Digital signatures give us an electronic way of achieving the same thing. Once a contract or agreement has been signed, neither party has a way of denying what was in the original terms of the contract.

There are many Internet websites that provide this service, with DocuSign being one of the most popular. In a service like this, the contract writer uploads the contract information, generally as a PDF, and it is sent to the recipient to sign. They put their electronic signature on the paper by clicking the signature field. In reality, the visual signature is not essential here; the cryptographic signing that takes place behind the scenes is important. Once the signee has signed the contract, the original sender, or a representative from that company, also endorses the contract. Once that has happened it means we have a countersigned, electronic document that is in possession of both parties.

If anyone tries to modify the terms of the contract, then when the agreement is electronically verified, none of the digital signatures will be correct, meaning tampering has occurred.

High-Level Look at Digital Signatures

Digital signatures are based on asymmetric cryptography. For the receiver of the message, a digital signature allows the receiver to believe the correct sender sent the message, this can be thought of as a digital equivalent to a signature on a letter, except a digital signature is much harder to forge.

Digital signatures give you both authentication and non-repudiation. Authentication because the signatures have to be created by a user with a valid private key, and non-repudiation as the receiver can trust that a known sender signed the message as only they know the private key. So, how do digital signatures do all this? Digital signatures in .NET and .NET Core are based on RSA, so some of the same rules for RSA apply for digital signatures. This is why you cannot sign data that is larger than the size of the key; that is, 1024 bits, 2048 bits, or 4096 bits. Because of this, it is common first to take a SHA-256 hash of the data that you want to sign digitally. You then use that hash to create the digital signature (see Figure 8-1).

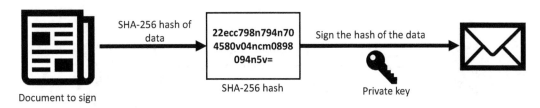

Figure 8-1. *Creating a digital signature from a hash of the original document*

A digital signature consists of the following three algorithms:

- Public and private key generation using RSA.

- A signing algorithm that uses the private key to create the signature.

- A signature verification algorithm that uses the public key to test if the message is authentic.

If you remember back to the last chapter where we talked about RSA, when you use RSA, to encrypt some data you use the recipient's public key, then the recipient uses their private key to decrypt the data. It is the other way around with digital signatures. The sender uses their private key to generate the signature, and the recipient uses the sender's public key to verify the signature, which is demonstrated in Table 8-1.

Table 8-1. *A Digital Signature Relies on the Private Key of the Sender*

	Public Key	Private Key
Encryption (RSA)	*Encrypt*	*Decrypt*
Digital signature	*Verify signature*	*Sign message*

Let's look at the process for creating a digital signature with the example shown in Figure 8-2.

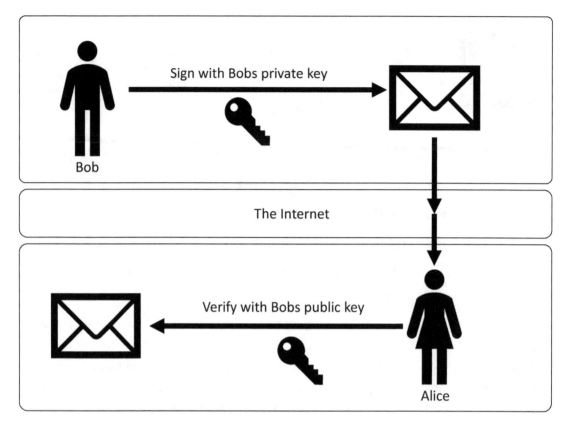

Figure 8-2. *The digital signing process from sender to receiver*

In the example, Bob is sending a message to Alice, and that message is signed with a digital signature.

First, Bob encrypts some data that he wants to send to Alice. For this example, it doesn't matter whether that data is encrypted with a symmetric or asymmetric encryption algorithm. Once this data is encrypted, Bob takes a SHA-256 hash of the data, where he signs the information with his private signing key; this creates the digital signature. Then Bob sends the encrypted data and the signature to Alice.

Once Alice has received the encrypted data and the digital signatures, she first recalculates the hash of the encrypted data (see Figure 8-3). Alice verifies the digital signature using the calculated hash and Bob's public signing key, which tells Alice if the signature is valid or not. If it is valid, Alice can be confident that Bob sent her the message because it could only have been signed using Bob's private signing key, which only Bob knows. If the signature is not valid, then Alice should not trust the origin and authenticity of the message and discard it entirely.

If Alice has a successfully verified the digital signature, she reads the message and decides to send a message and signature back to Bob. She does this using the same process. Let's walk through it.

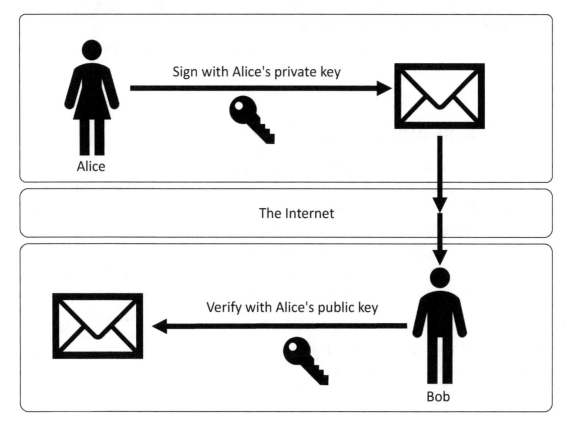

Figure 8-3. *The receiver of a digital signature verifying the signature*

First Alice encrypts some data that she wants to send to Bob. Once this data has been encrypted, Alice takes a hash of that data and then she signs the hash with her private signing key; this creates the digital signature. Then Alice sends the encrypted data and the signature to Bob.

First, Bob recalculates the hash of the encrypted data. Bob verifies the digital signature using the calculated hash and Alice's public signing key. This tells Bob if the signature is valid or not. If it is valid, Bob can be confident that it was Alice that sent him the message because it could only have been signed using her private signing key, which only Alice knows. If the signature is not valid, then Bob should not trust the origin and authenticity of the message.

As illustrated in the two-way communication between Bob and Alice, it is because we sign with the senders' private key that the recipient can trust the message as only the sender should know the private key. Naturally, this means the sender is responsible for making sure that their private key is safe and secure. I cover that in more detail later in the book when we look at Azure Key Vault.

Now that we have looked at how a digital signature works in theory, let's now look at how it is implemented in the .NET Framework/.NET Core.

Digital Signatures in .NET

The digital signatures implementation that we are going to use in .NET is based on RSA and enables us to perform the same key generation techniques as we discussed in the last chapter. There is no difference in the key generation; the only difference is what the keys are used for. We sign data using the private key and verify it with the public key. All the key creation techniques work just fine, like the in-memory keys with RSAParameters, the XML-based keys, and the CSP keys. Only the RSAParameters version of the key generation code works across Windows, macOS, and Linux under .NET Core, so that is what we use in the following code, which is the same as we used in Chapter 7.

```
private RSAParameters _publicKey;
private RSAParameters _privateKey;

public void AssignNewKey()
{
    using (var rsa = new RSACryptoServiceProvider(2048))
    {
        rsa.PersistKeyInCsp = false;
        _publicKey = rsa.ExportParameters(false);
        _privateKey = rsa.ExportParameters(true);
    }
}
```

Apart from the key generation, a digital signature in .NET/.NET Core requires two further classes to work in addition to RSACryptoServiceProvider. These classes are RSAPKCS1SignatureFormatter and RSAPKCS1SignatureDeformatter, which sign and verify our data, respectively.

```
public byte[] SignData(byte[] hashOfDataToSign)
{
    using (var rsa = new RSACryptoServiceProvider())
    {
        rsa.PersistKeyInCsp = false;
        rsa.ImportParameters(_privateKey);

        var rsaFormatter = new RSAPKCS1SignatureFormatter(rsa);

        rsaFormatter.SetHashAlgorithm("SHA256");

        return rsaFormatter.CreateSignature(hashOfDataToSign);
    }
}
```

In the preceding code example, you can see that the RSACryptoServiceProvider
class is first constructed with a key size of 2048, and you then import your private key,
which you have already created. Then the RSAPKCS1SignatureFormatter object is
created, and you pass in the rsa object containing the private key. Alternatively, you
can create the RSAPKCS1SignatureFormatter with the default constructor and then call
SetKey by passing in the rsa object.

Once the RSAPKCS1SignatureFormatter class has been instantiated, you then set the
hashing algorithm that is going to be used in the signature creation process. The hash
name has to be configured as a string.

The valid options are

- MD5

- SHA-1

- SHA-256

- SHA-512

Our example uses SHA-256. Once a hash algorithm has been set, you can call
CreateSignature and pass in a hash of the data that you want to sign, which needs to be
passed in as a byte array. Once CreateSignature has been called, it gives you back a byte
array containing your digital signature.

```
public bool VerifySignature(byte[] hashOfDataToSign,
                            byte[] signature)
{
    using (var rsa = new RSACryptoServiceProvider())
    {
        rsa.ImportParameters(_publicKey);

        var rsaDeformatter = new RSAPKCS1SignatureDeformatter(rsa);

        rsaDeformatter.SetHashAlgorithm("SHA256");

        return rsaDeformatter.VerifySignature(
                        hashOfDataToSign, signature);
    }
}
```

Verifying a digital signature is a similar process to creating a signature, the only difference, as you can see in the preceding code, is that instead of importing the private key, you import the public key. Instead of using the RSAPKCS1SignatureFormatter class, you use RSAPKCS1SignatureDeformatter. To verify the digital signature, you call VerifySignature and pass in the hash of the data that you want to verify and the actual signature that was returned from the SignData method.

If the hash that is provided doesn't match what was used to create the original digital signature, then you get false returned from VerifySignature. Let's think about that in practical terms. Bob has a PDF contract that he is sending to Alice, so he creates a hash of the PDF, and then creates the digital signature of that hash using his private key. Bob then sends the digital signature and the PDF file to Alice. Alice recalculates the hash of the PDF and passes that hash and Bobs digital signatures into VerifySignature, and if it returns true, then she trusts the integrity of the document that was sent, and she trusts that it came from Bob as he used his private key to create the digital signature.

Let's now assume that after Bob sent the PDF and the digital signature, it was all intercepted by Eve, and she edits the PDF and changes some of the information within it. When they finally get to Alice, she recalculates the hash code for the PDF and calls VerifySignature with the new hash code and the original digital signature. This time it returns false, which means that she should not trust the document. Alice can't trust the integrity of the file or the origin of the digital signature.

In the following code, we try our digital signature implementation.

```
static void Main(string[] args)
{
    var document = Encoding.UTF8.GetBytes("Document to Sign");
    byte[] hashedDocument;

    using (var sha256 = SHA256.Create())
    {
        hashedDocument = sha256.ComputeHash(document);
    }

    var digitalSignature = new DigitalSignature();
    digitalSignature.AssignNewKey();

    var signature = digitalSignature.SignData(hashedDocument);

    var verified = digitalSignature.VerifySignature(
                                hashedDocument, signature);

    Console.WriteLine("Digital Signature Demonstration in .NET");
    Console.WriteLine("---------------------------------------");
    Console.WriteLine("    Original Text = " +
                        Encoding.Default.GetString(document));

    Console.WriteLine();
    Console.WriteLine("    Digital Signature = " +
                        Convert.ToBase64String(signature));

    Console.WriteLine(verified
        ? "The digital signature has been correctly verified."
        : "The digital signature has NOT been correctly verified.");
}
```

First, we have our document that we want to sign digitally. In our example, it is a string, but it could just as easily be a file that you have loaded into a byte array.

```
var document = Encoding.UTF8.GetBytes("Document to Sign");
byte[] hashedDocument;

using (var sha256 = SHA256.Create())
```

```
{
    hashedDocument = sha256.ComputeHash(document);
}
```

First, we need to convert our document into a byte array and then create an SHA-256 hash of the document using the same technique that we explored in our chapter on hashing.

```
var digitalSignature = new DigitalSignature();
digitalSignature.AssignNewKey();

var signature = digitalSignature.SignData(hashedDocument);
var verified = digitalSignature.VerifySignature(hashedDocument, signature);
```

Next, we create an instance of our DigitalSignature class that contains our AssignNewKey, SignData, and VerifySignature methods. Once the class has been instantiated, we create new keys by calling the AssignNewKey method. I discuss better ways of managing these signing keys later in the book.

Next, we call SignData and pass in the hash of the document, which returns our digital signature as a byte array. Immediately afterward, we call VerifySignature to check that it is valid, which it should be because we have not changed the original document or hash. You can see the result of this in Figure 8-4.

Figure 8-4. *The result of a new digital signature and its verification*

If you are using the code samples that come with this book, try running the digital signature code in the debugger, but stop at a breakpoint when you have created the digital signature. Then open up the byte array of the hashedDocument and change one of the bytes to something else, as you can see in Figure 8-5.

```
using (var sha256 = SHA256.Create())
{
    hashedDocument = sha256.ComputeHash(document);
}

var digitalSignature = new DigitalSignature
digitalSignature.AssignNewKey();

var signature = digitalSignature.SignData(h
var verified = digitalSignature.VerifySigna

Console.WriteLine("Digital Signature Demons
Console.WriteLine("----------------------
Console.WriteLine();
Console.WriteLine();
Console.WriteLine("   Original Text = " +
```

hashedDocument	{byte[32]}
[0]	29
[1]	232
[2]	194
[3]	49
[4]	145
[5]	59
[6]	107

Figure 8-5. *Modifying a document after the digital signature has been created*

When you have modified the hashedDocument variable contents, let the debugger continue past the call to VerifySignature. Here you see that VerifySignature returns false. If you allow the program to complete, you see the output shown in Figure 8-6 in your terminal window.

```
● ● ● ⌃ stephenhaunts — DigitalSignature.dll — dotnet ‹ bash -c clear; cd "/Applicatio...

Digital Signature Demonstration in .NET
----------------------------------------


   Original Text = Document to Sign

   Digital Signature = JSsbMTKpAtpjD0T//vPaHFEcGqggMCssovqcV3Akntxh41v4/atSMDXOz
5nUrLzvFwB+iamBfH+cS5Pljh3P1ZVHq6tQ+JG9galgiZjs/ehJxoU6/Ja41p/Qb25goUEfDDTMCsAAs
crI9FvGHw15WWFxSakfxlgfvscn7pphZ8LxfJPJd0FY79kYPG95JKJfv8Rt5IuEEHaCB3q1TG4m00A4X
n1zBRs1K4fQJiQBXlc7rLe7VxMmQF8dREcSDOOfnirex71POybHQLDLpZ86cXA0htiamaMrJf+iFnNVb
39xh/4m37s9pns8mvRR6dFD6aQiQ3v1pAYA/Mpk/R0+EA==

The digital signature has NOT been correctly verified.
▮
```

Figure 8-6. *The digital signature does not match the modified document*

This example demonstrates that if the document is tampered with and a new hash calculated, it will not match the original digital signature. This is a powerful property that we explore when I talk about hybrid encryption in Chapter 9.

Summary

In this chapter, we explored the final pillar of our four cryptographic pillars, which was non-repudiation. Non-repudiation is where the receiver of the message cannot deny that the message is authentic. We get the authenticity due to the fact that the message sender has to use their private key to create a digital signature, and only they know their private key, so when the recipient verifies the signature using the recipient public key, they can be assured that the signature is valid if the signature verifier returns true.

We have now covered all the primitives needed to satisfy our four pillars of cryptography. Each of these primitives is incredibly useful on their own, but when we start to combine them we can get some compelling benefits, and this is what we are going to explore in our next chapter on hybrid cryptography.

CHAPTER 9

Hybrid Encryption

At the beginning of the book, I discussed four security principles to tackle with cryptography in our software solutions (see Figure 9-1). Let's review them.

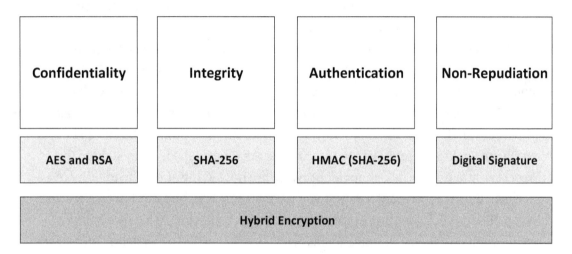

Figure 9-1. *Cryptographic primitives to be used for hybrid encryption*

First, confidentiality is what you traditionally associate with cryptography, which is where you take a message or some other data and encrypt it to make the original data completely unreadable. There are many cryptography algorithms, including symmetric encryption with DES, Triple DES, and AES. We also covered asymmetric encryption using RSA.

The second type of security operation is integrity. In information security, data integrity means maintaining and assuring the accuracy and consistency of data over its entire lifecycle; this means that data cannot be modified in an unauthorized or undetected manner. Integrity is violated when a message is actively changed in transit. Systems typically provide message integrity in addition to data confidentiality. We covered different techniques for giving integrity with our look at MD5, SHA-1, SHA-256,

© Stephen Haunts 2019
S. Haunts, *Applied Cryptography in .NET and Azure Key Vault*,
https://doi.org/10.1007/978-1-4842-4375-6_9

and SHA-512. We also covered hashed message authentication codes (HMACs) that also make use of MD5, SHA-1, SHA-256, and SHA-512. HMAC's form the third pillar of cryptography.

The fourth type of security pillar is that of Non-Repudiation. Non-repudiation is the assurance that someone cannot deny something happening. Non-repudiation gives you the ability to make sure that one of the parties to a contract cannot end up rejecting the authenticity of their signature on the contract. Non-repudiation also means that the sender of a contract cannot deny that the message originated from them. Another good example is where you send a letter or parcel by recorded delivery which means the recipient has to sign for the shipment which means they cannot deny their package was delivered. Similarly, a legal document typically requires witnesses to its signing so that the person who signs it cannot deny having done so.

In the digital age, a digital signature ensures that a message has been signed by the person who claimed to sign the message. One person can only create the digital signature, and this ensures that person cannot deny that they signed the message.

The fifth pillar of cryptography is authentication. A good example of authentication is when we want to establish the identity of a server using an SSL or TLS certificate. A certificate enables us to prove identity to a user that he or she is connected to the correct server. When we talk about identity, we are not talking about the identity of a direct user, that a cryptographic key. If you have a weak key, then this lowers the trust that you place on that identity. Authentication is also commonly used by everyone when they enter their user name and password to gain access to a system. Your social media accounts are an excellent example of this. To interact with your friends, you have to authenticate yourself with the social media website to prove who you are. We investigated authentication when we looked at the secure storage of passwords, by using a hashing, salting, and time delaying scheme that would guard against Moore's law and the ever-increasing speed and power of computer processors. The technique we looked at was using a password-based key derivation functions.

Now we want to combine some of the techniques to create an encryption system that is powerful and flexible. We start by combining the best of both worlds of symmetric and asymmetric encryption.

Combining Symmetric and Asymmetric

Symmetric encryption with algorithms, such as DES, Triple DES, and AES, are fast and efficient when it comes to encrypting data, but the problem with symmetric encryption is sharing keys. Sharing keys securely between two or more people is very hard to do.

For asymmetric encryption, the actual process of encryption is much slower due to the modular-based mathematical nature of the RSA, and there are limits to the amount of data that you can encrypt at once. A real benefit for RSA is how keys are managed. With RSA, you use a public and private key pair. The recipient of the message knows the private key, and they keep that key safe and secret; anyone can know the public key. If Alice wants to send a message to Bob, she first gets his public key; encrypts the message with that public key and sends the message to Bob. Bob then uses his private key to read the message; which is a much better solution to keys exchange than with symmetric encryption algorithms like AES.

What we want to do now, is get the best of both worlds. We want the fast and efficient encryption properties of AES coupled with the more robust key sharing mechanism of RSA (see Figure 9-2). We are going to look at *hybrid encryption*, which is achieved using unique symmetric session keys along with asymmetric encryption.

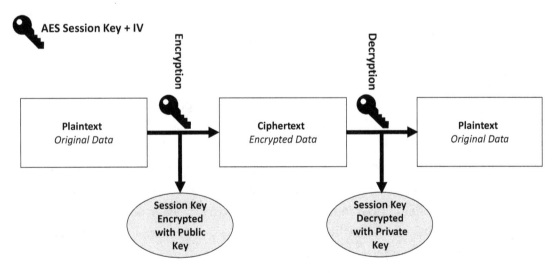

Figure 9-2. *Using RSA to protect our AES session key*

The sender first uses the recipient's public key to encrypt a freshly generated AES session key. The data you want to send to the recipient is encrypted with AES and that session key, and that encrypted message along with the RSA encrypted session key is sent to the recipient who then uses their private key to decrypt the session key. Once the session key is recovered, it is then used to decrypt the message.

The combination of encryption methods has various advantages. One is that a connection channel is established between two users' sets of equipment. Users then can communicate using this hybrid encryption technique. A downside of asymmetric encryption is that it can slow down the encryption process, but with using it along with symmetric encryption, both of them together use their best parts, the efficiency of the symmetric encryption and the key splitting of the asymmetric encryption. The result is added security to the message sending process along with overall improved system performance.

Let's run through this step by step, as shown in Figure 9-3.

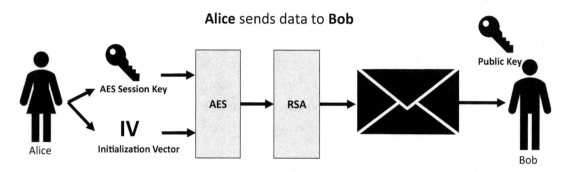

Figure 9-3. *Alice sends Bob a message using RSA and AES*

We have two people: Alice and Bob.

First, **Alice** sends a message to **Bob** using hybrid encryption.

Alice generates a 256-bit (32-byte) AES key. This key is called a *session key* in this process.

Alice then generates a 128-bit (16-byte) initialization vector (IV). The IV is a block of random data that is passed into the AES algorithm to add additional entropy to the encryption process. Remember that the IV doesn't have to be kept secret.

Alice encrypts her message with AES using the session key and the IV, which is the same as any normal encryption operation with AES.

Alice then encrypts the session key with RSA and **Bob's** public key. Here we are wrapping the AES session key with the strength of RSA. If anyone wants to decrypt the original message with AES, they first need to decrypt this RSA encrypted key with **Bob's** private key.

Alice stores the encrypted data, encrypted AES session key, and IV in a separate structure or file, which is the packet of data that is sent to **Bob**. Now **Bob** has this packet of information he wants to decrypt it. This is illustrated in Figure 9-4.

Encrypted Data Packet

RSA Encrypted Session Key
AES Initialization Vector
AES Encrypted Data

Figure 9-4. *The packet of data containing everything needed to decrypt the message*

To decrypt the data, **Bob** performs the process shown in Figure 9-5.

Bob reads the decrypted message

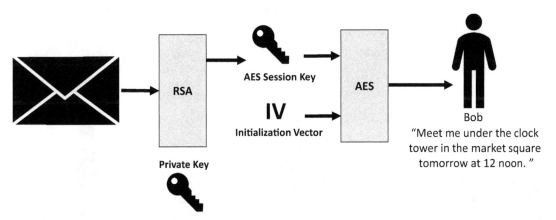

Figure 9-5. *The process for Bob to decrypt the message*

Bob first decrypts the encrypted AES session key with RSA and his private key.

Bob decrypts the encrypted data by using the recovered AES session key and the original IV that was sent to him.

Bob reads his decrypted message. The message says, "Meet me under the clock tower in the market square tomorrow at 12 noon."

Let's run through this example again for clarity, but this time, **Bob** is going to send a reply back to **Alice**. This is shown in Figure 9-6.

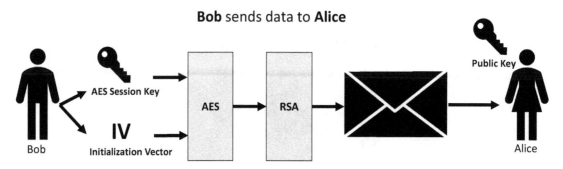

Figure 9-6. *Bob sends a reply to Alice using the same process*

Bob generates a 256-bit (32-byte) AES Key which is our session key.

Bob generates a 128-bit (16-byte) IV.

Bob encrypts his reply to **Alice** with AES by using the session key and the IV.

Bob encrypts the AES session key with RSA and **Alice's** public key.

Bob stores the encrypted data, encrypted AES session key, and IV in a separate data structure which is the packet of data that is sent to **Alice**.

Now that **Alice** has received the message from **Bob**, she decrypts it with the process shown in Figure 9-7.

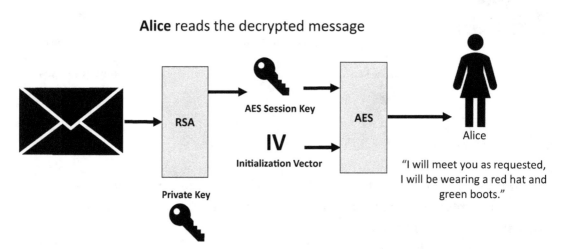

Figure 9-7. *Alice decrypts the message from Bob*

Alice decrypts the encrypted AES session key by using RSA and her private key.

Alice decrypts the encrypted message from **Bob** by using decrypted AES session key and the IV.

Alice reads the decrypted message, which says, "I will meet you as requested. I will be wearing a red hat and green boots."

Let's now put this into practice with a code demonstration. Before we look specifically at the hybrid encryption example, let's review the AES and RSA implementations that we will use. To cover our symmetric encryption needs, we have a class called AesEncryption that contains three methods. The first is GenerateRandomNumber, which we use for creating symmetric keys and IVs. The method takes a length as a parameter, which is the length in bytes that we want to key to be, and then the method returns us a byte array of the desired length containing the random number.

The next method is our Encrypt method which takes a byte array of the data we want to encrypt, a byte array containing our key (32 bytes for our example) and the IV, which is 16 bytes. Once our data has been encrypted, the ciphertext is returned as a byte array.

Finally, the Decrypt method takes a byte array of our ciphertext, a byte array of our symmetric key, and a byte array of our IV. Once the data has been decrypted, the plaintext byte array is returned. These three short methods cover our symmetric encryption needs.

```
public class AesEncryption
{
    public byte[] GenerateRandomNumber(int length)
    {
        using (var randomNumberGenerator =
                    new RNGCryptoServiceProvider())
        {
            var randomNumber = new byte[length];
            randomNumberGenerator.GetBytes(randomNumber);

            return randomNumber;
        }
    }

    public byte[] Encrypt(byte[] dataToEncrypt,
                        byte[] key, byte[] iv)
```

```csharp
    {
        using (var aes = new AesCryptoServiceProvider())
        {
            aes.Mode = CipherMode.CBC;
            aes.Padding = PaddingMode.PKCS7;

            aes.Key = key;
            aes.IV = iv;

            using (var memoryStream = new MemoryStream())
            {
                var cryptoStream =
                    new CryptoStream(memoryStream,
                                     aes.CreateEncryptor(),
                                     CryptoStreamMode.Write);

                cryptoStream.Write(dataToEncrypt, 0,
                                   dataToEncrypt.Length);

                cryptoStream.FlushFinalBlock();

                return memoryStream.ToArray();
            }
        }
    }

    public byte[] Decrypt(byte[] dataToDecrypt,
                          byte[] key, byte[] iv)
    {
        using (var aes = new AesCryptoServiceProvider())
        {
            aes.Mode = CipherMode.CBC;
            aes.Padding = PaddingMode.PKCS7;

            aes.Key = key;
            aes.IV = iv;

            using (var memoryStream = new MemoryStream())
            {
```

```
                var cryptoStream =
                    new CryptoStream(memoryStream,
                                    aes.CreateDecryptor(),
                                     CryptoStreamMode.Write);

            cryptoStream.Write(dataToDecrypt, 0,
                                dataToDecrypt.Length);

            cryptoStream.FlushFinalBlock();

            var decryptBytes = memoryStream.ToArray();
            return decryptBytes;
        }
    }
  }
}
```

For our asymmetric encryption needs, we are using RSA, and more specifically for this example, the RSA with parameter keys version that stores the public and private key pairs as in-memory objects. Later in the book, we look at a more robust way of managing the RSA keys.

The RSAWithRSAParameterKey class contains three methods; the first of which is AssignNewKey, which generates our public and private key pair. Our example code is set to create 2048-bit keys, which are strong at the time this book goes to press. You can go higher to 4096-bit keys if you wish, but you will suffer a performance penalty.

The next method is EncryptData, which takes a byte array of our plaintext as it's the only parameter. EncryptData loads the public key and then encrypts the data, where the ciphertext is returned as a byte array to the caller.

The final method is called DecryptData, which takes a byte array of our ciphertext. DecryptData loads up the private key and then decrypts the data, where the plaintext is returned as a byte array to the caller.

```
public class RSAWithRSAParameterKey
{
    private RSAParameters _publicKey;
    private RSAParameters _privateKey;

    public void AssignNewKey()
```

```
    {
        using (var rsa = new RSACryptoServiceProvider(2048))
        {
            rsa.PersistKeyInCsp = false;
            _publicKey = rsa.ExportParameters(false);
            _privateKey = rsa.ExportParameters(true);
        }
    }

    public byte[] EncryptData(byte[] dataToEncrypt)
    {
        byte[] cipherbytes;

        using (var rsa = new RSACryptoServiceProvider())
        {
            rsa.PersistKeyInCsp = false;
            rsa.ImportParameters(_publicKey);

            cipherbytes = rsa.Encrypt(dataToEncrypt, true);
        }

        return cipherbytes;
    }

    public byte[] DecryptData(byte[] dataToEncrypt)
    {
        byte[] plain;

        using (var rsa = new RSACryptoServiceProvider())
        {
            rsa.PersistKeyInCsp = false;

            rsa.ImportParameters(_privateKey);
            plain = rsa.Decrypt(dataToEncrypt, true);
        }

        return plain;
    }
}
```

Our AesEncryption and RSAWithRSAParameterKey classes are the two primitives that we need for our first pass at a hybrid encryption scheme, which gives us confidentiality. First, we need to store our encrypted data. For that, we define a class called EncryptedPacket. This class contains everything that the sender of our hybrid encrypted message needs to send to the recipient. First, there is a byte array containing the encrypted session key, and this is safe to send because the original session key was encrypted with RSA. Next, we have a byte array containing the encrypted data, which is the data that is encrypted with AES using the session key. Finally, we have a byte array that contains our IV. Remember, we need this additional piece of entropy to pass into the first AES encryption block, but the IV doesn't have to be kept secret, so we can send it as is.

```
public class EncryptedPacket
{
    public byte[] EncryptedSessionKey;
    public byte[] EncryptedData;
    public byte[] Iv;
}
```

Now that we have somewhere to store our encrypted data, we need some code to implement our hybrid encryption scheme. The sample code for this book defines a class called HybridEncryption, and to start within this class we define a read-only instance of our AesEncryption class.

```
private readonly AesEncryption _aes = new AesEncryption();

public EncryptedPacket EncryptData(byte[] original,
                        RSAWithRSAParameterKey rsaParams)
{
    var sessionKey = _aes.GenerateRandomNumber(32);

    var encryptedPacket = new EncryptedPacket
        {
            Iv = _aes.GenerateRandomNumber(16)
        };

    encryptedPacket.EncryptedData = _aes.Encrypt(original, sessionKey,
                                encryptedPacket.Iv);
```

```
encryptedPacket.EncryptedSessionKey =
                    rsaParams.EncryptData(sessionKey);

    return encryptedPacket;
}
```

Then the EncryptData method performs the hybrid encrypt. This method takes a byte array containing our plaintext and an instance of the RSAWithRSAParameterKey class that contains our predefined public and private key. The EncryptData method first starts by generating the 32-byte AES session key. Next, an instance of the EncryptedPacket is created, and the 16-byte IV is generated and stored in the IV field of the EncryptedPacket instance.

The next step is to encrypt our plaintext data using AES and the newly generated session key. The result of this is stored in the EncryptedData field of the EncryptedPacket. The next step is to encrypt the AES session key then using RSA; this is done by calling the EncryptData method on the RSAWithRSAParameterKey instance that was passed into our hybrid encryption method. This encryption operation uses the public key, and when the AES session key is encrypted, it is stored in the EncryptedPacket instance, which can then be sent to the recipient.

Let's now look at the decryption operation.

```
public byte[] DecryptData(EncryptedPacket encryptedPacket,
                    RSAWithRSAParameterKey rsaParams)
{

    var decryptedSessionKey =
            rsaParams.DecryptData(
                    encryptedPacket.EncryptedSessionKey);

    var decryptedData = _aes.Decrypt(
                    encryptedPacket.EncryptedData,
                    decryptedSessionKey, encryptedPacket.Iv);

    return decryptedData;
}
```

The DecryptData method takes two parameters; the first is the EncryptedPacket object that has been sent by the sender, and this contains the encrypted AES session key, the encrypted message, and the IV. The second parameter contains the RSA keys, the private key which is used in this decryption method.

Before we can do anything, we first have to recover the encrypted AES session key; this is done by calling DecryptData on our rsaParams parameter, which decrypts the session key using the RSA private key of the recipient. Now that we recovered the session key, and have the IV, we can use AES to decrypt our encrypted message from the sender, which returns the original ciphertext as a byte array.

We have now implemented a simple scheme to use the efficiency of AES to encrypt our data, but the split key properties of RSA to exchange our encrypted message without compromising any keys. Let's look at calling this from a sample application.

```
static void Main(string[] args)
{
    const string original = "Very secret and important information that can
    not fall into the wrong hands.";

    var rsaParams = new RSAWithRSAParameterKey();
    rsaParams.AssignNewKey();

    var hybrid = new HybridEncryption();

    var encryptedBlock = hybrid.EncryptData(
            Encoding.UTF8.GetBytes(original), rsaParams);

    var decrpyted = hybrid.DecryptData(encryptedBlock,
                                        rsaParams);

    Console.WriteLine("Hybrid Encryption Demonstration");
    Console.WriteLine("-------------------------------");
    Console.WriteLine();
    Console.WriteLine("Original Message = " + original);
    Console.WriteLine();
    Console.WriteLine("Message After Decryption = "
                + Encoding.UTF8.GetString(decrpyted));
    Console.ReadLine();
}
```

First, we define the message we want to encrypt. In this case, it is a string, but it could as easily be a file. Next, we create an instance of the RSAWithRSAParameterKey class and then call AssignNewKey, which generates a public and private key pair. Then, we create an instance of the HybridEncryption class and then call the EncryptData method on it. We pass in the message to encrypt (converted to a byte array first), and the class instance, rsaParams, containing our RSA key pair. We are left with an instance of our EncryptedPacket object containing the encrypted session key, encrypted data, and IV. To decrypt the data, we call the DecryptData method on the HybridEncryption class instance and provide the encrypted packet and the RSAWithRSAParameterKey class instance that contains our private key. Once the plaintext byte array is returned, it is turned back into a string and displayed to the console.

The results can be seen in Figure 9-8. You see the message before it was encrypted and the message after it was decrypted to prove that our hybrid encryption scheme is working.

```
stephenhaunts — Visual Studio External Console — dotnet · bash -c clear; cd "/Us...

Hybrid Encryption Demonstration in .NET
-------------------------------------------

Original Message = Very secret and important information that can not fall into the
 wrong hands.

Message After Decryption = Very secret and important information that can not fall
into the wrong hands.
```

Figure 9-8. *The results of running our first hybrid encryption example*

Adding Integrity Checks

Now that we have started our hybrid encryption example, we have covered the confidentiality security requirement by incorporating symmetric and asymmetric encryption. To extend the example, let's add integrity checking to the code to ensure that the message that Alice sends to Bob is not corrupted or tampered with in transit.

The simplest way to do this is by taking a hash of the encrypted data and the IV. This could be done using any of the hashing operations, such as MD5, SHA-1, or SHA-2.

The hash is calculated after the message has been encrypted with AES and sent to the recipient inside the encrypted packet, as shown in Figure 9-9.

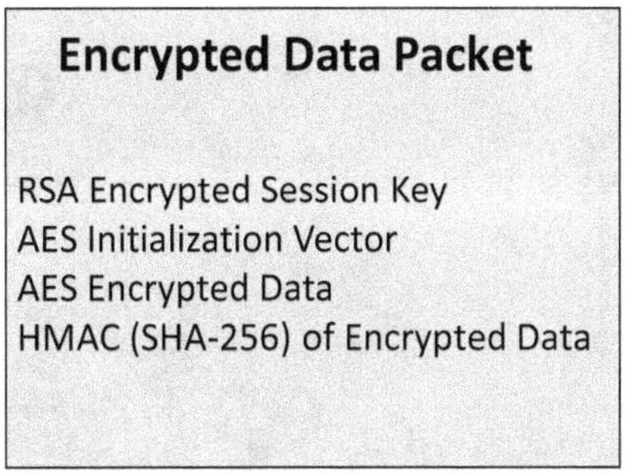

Encrypted Data Packet

RSA Encrypted Session Key
AES Initialization Vector
AES Encrypted Data
HMAC (SHA-256) of Encrypted Data

Figure 9-9. *The encrypted packet of data containing the new HMAC*

When the recipient wants to decrypt the message, they first recalculate the hash of the encrypted message and IV. If the hashes match, then the data is intact and hasn't been corrupted or tampered with, which means the recipient can safely decrypt the message. If the hash codes do not match, then there has been an issue during transmission of the message; it has either been corrupted or tampered with. The recipient should not trust it and discard the message entirely.

As a solution, this works quite well, but we can go one better. With this solution of hashing the encrypted data and IV, nothing is stopping an attacker intercepting the message, corrupting the encrypted data or IV and then recalculating the hash. It would be much better if the strength of our session key could also protect the hashing of the data; this is possible by a hashed message authentication code or HMAC like we discussed in Chapter 4.

Like plain hash code, HMACs are used to verify the integrity of a message. HMACs also allows you to verify the authentication of that message because only the person who knows the private key to recover the session key can calculate the same hash of the message. Without that session key, you cannot recalculate the same hash code of the encrypted data. HMACs can be used with different hashing functions, such as MD5 or the SHA family of algorithms. In the examples in the rest of this chapter, we use SHA-256. The cryptographic strength of HMACs depends on the size of the key that is used.

Let's look at one of our previous examples and incorporate the HMAC into it. This is illustrated in Figure 9-10.

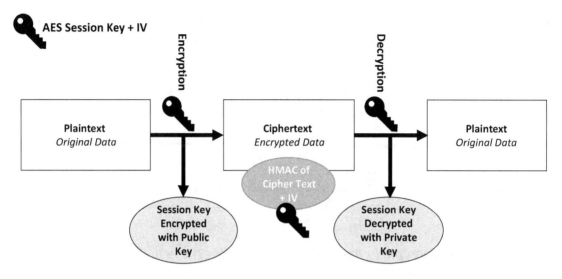

Figure 9-10. *The hybrid encryption process incorporating HMAC for integrity*

First, **Alice** is going to send a message to **Bob** using hybrid encryption with built-in integrity checking.

Alice generates a new 256-bit (32-byte) AES session key. When establishing a communication channel like this, you should never reuse the same key.

Alice generates a new 128-bit (16-byte) IV; again, as with the session key, you should never reuse the same IV. The IV is a block of random data that is passed into the AES algorithm to add additional entropy to the encryption process; remember that the IV doesn't have to be kept secret.

Alice then encrypts her message with AES using the session key and the IV.

Alice encrypts the session key with RSA and **Bob's** public key. Here we are again wrapping the AES session key with the strength of RSA. If anyone wants to decrypt the original message with AES, they first need to decrypt this RSA encrypted key with the private key which should only be known to **Bob**.

Alice then calculates the HMAC of the encrypted data and IV combined using the unencrypted AES session key as the key for the HMAC which means that the recipient can only recalculate the same hash once they have decrypted the AES session key with their private key.

Alice stores the encrypted message, encrypted AES session key, IV and HMAC in a separate structure or file to send to **Bob**.

Now **Bob** has this packet of information he wants to decrypt it.

To do this, he uses the following process.

Bob decrypts the encrypted AES session key by using RSA and his private key.

Bob recalculates the HMAC of the encrypted data and IV using the decrypted AES session key.

Bob compares his HMAC to the HMAC sent with the message. If the HMACs match, then the data is intact and hasn't been corrupted, and it is safe to decrypt the message. If the HMACs do not match, then we don't have message integrity, and the message should be discarded.

If the HMACs match, then **Bob** decrypts the encrypted data by using the decrypted AES session key and the IV.

Bob reads the decrypted message.

Let's now show this in practice in the next code demonstration. The first update we want to make is to the EncryptedPacket class, where we added a new byte array field called Hmac that is going to store the HMAC of the encrypted data and the IV.

```
public class EncryptedPacket
{
    public byte[] EncryptedSessionKey;
    public byte[] EncryptedData;
    public byte[] Iv;
    public byte[] Hmac;
}
```

Next, we want to extend the EncryptData method in our HybridEncryption class. The following code is identical to the code we looked at in our first hybrid encryption example except for the addition at the bottom of the method that has been highlighted in bold.

```
private readonly AesEncryption _aes = new AesEncryption();

public EncryptedPacket EncryptData(byte[] original,
                        RSAWithRSAParameterKey rsaParams)
{
    var sessionKey = _aes.GenerateRandomNumber(32);
    var encryptedPacket = new EncryptedPacket
      {
          Iv = _aes.GenerateRandomNumber(16)
      };
```

```
encryptedPacket.EncryptedData = _aes.Encrypt(original, sessionKey,
                                  encryptedPacket.Iv);

encryptedPacket.EncryptedSessionKey = rsaParams.EncryptData(sessionKey);

using (var hmac = new HMACSHA256(sessionKey))
{
    encryptedPacket.Hmac = hmac.ComputeHash(
                  Combine(encryptedPacket.EncryptedData,
                      encryptedPacket.Iv));
}

return encryptedPacket;
}
```

Once the session key has been created, the IV set, our message encrypted with AES and our session key encrypted with RSA; the next step is to create our HMAC. First, an instance is created for the HMACSHA256 class, and we pass in our session key. It makes sense to use the HMAC over a straight SHA-256 hash because we already have our session key, which means the recipient needs to recover the session key before recalculating the HMAC.

The HMAC is created by passing in the encrypted data and the IV combined; this means those two-byte arrays need to be appended together. You can do this with the following code which creates a new byte array of the desired length and then uses the Buffer.BlockCopy operation to copy the source byte arrays into the new byte array.

```
private static byte[] Combine(byte[] first, byte[] second)
{
    var ret = new byte[first.Length + second.Length];

    Buffer.BlockCopy(first, 0, ret, 0, first.Length);

    Buffer.BlockCopy(second, 0, ret, first.Length, second.Length);

    return ret;
}
```

Once the HMAC has been calculated it is put into our **EncryptedPacket** object. Now let's look at the decryption operation. The majority of this decryption method is the same as the previous hybrid encryption example, but the additions are highlighted in bold.

```
public byte[] DecryptData(EncryptedPacket encryptedPacket,
                          RSAWithRSAParameterKey rsaParams)
{
    var decryptedSessionKey = rsaParams.DecryptData(
                        encryptedPacket.EncryptedSessionKey);

    using (var hmac = new HMACSHA256(decryptedSessionKey))
    {
        var hmacToCheck = hmac.ComputeHash(
                Combine(encryptedPacket.EncryptedData,
                        encryptedPacket.Iv));

        if (!Compare(encryptedPacket.Hmac, hmacToCheck))
        {
            throw new CryptographicException(
              "HMAC does not match encrypted packet.");
        }
    }

    var decryptedData = _aes.Decrypt(
            encryptedPacket.EncryptedData,
            decryptedSessionKey,
            encryptedPacket.Iv);

    return decryptedData;
}
```

Once the session key has been decrypted with RSA, the first thing we want to do is check the integrity of our message. First, we create an instance of the HMACSHA256 class and provide it with our recovered session key. Then we want to calculate a new version of the HMAC that was provided in the encrypted packet; this means we combine the encrypted data and the IV again and then create the HMAC of the result.

Next, we compare the HMAC we just created to the HMAC that we were sent in the encrypted packet. If they do not match then we throw an exception and abort the method as this means the integrity of the encrypted data and the IV has been compromised, and we don't trust the message. If they do match, then we can go ahead and decrypt our message as we trust that the data hasn't been tampered with or corrupted.

This example extends our previous hybrid encryption example, which gave us confidentiality, with both integrity and authentication. We get integrity from the fact we are calculating and storing a hash for the encrypted data and IV, and we get authentication from the fact we used a hashed message authentication code instead of a standard hash. Utilizing the HMAC means that we need to provide the key to the hashing operation, which in our case is the unencrypted session key. This key needs to be decrypted using the RSA private key before the HMAC can be calculated to get a matching hash code.

Securely Comparing Byte Arrays

When dealing with byte arrays, it is common to want to check if one array is the same as another. We did this in the previous example by comparing the byte arrays of two HMAC hashes. Typically, you might have an implementation like the following.

```
private static bool CompareUnSecure(
                    byte[] array1, byte[] array2)
{
    if (array1.Length != array2.Length)
    {
        return false;
    }

    for (int i = 0; i < array1.Length; ++i)
    {
        if (array1[i] != array2[i])
        {
            return false;
        }
    }

    return true;
}
```

In this example, the Compare method takes two-byte arrays and returns true if they are equal and false otherwise. This works by first checking if the array lengths are the same. If they are not, the method returns false. It then iterates through the first array and checks each element of the array against the second array. If it finds an item that is not equal, it returns false.

On the surface of it, this sounds like a reasonable implementation and efficient because it aborts as soon as it detects that the arrays are different. However, when dealing with cryptographic processes, this isn't such a good idea. A potential attacker can use this type of comparison as a vulnerability and perform a *side-channel timing attack*, which uses information from a physical implementation of a cryptosystem, instead of from a brute force or theoretical weaknesses in the algorithms. For example, you could use timing information, electromagnetic interference, or power consumption, or sound as a way to gain extra insight, which can help an attacker exploit a system.

In our example, which compares a byte array, an attacker can glean information from the method because it executes at different times based on the arrays that are fed into it. Ideally, you need a Compare method that executes at the same time no matter how equal (or not) the arrays are.

A better implementation uses something like the following.

```
private static bool Compare(byte[] array1, byte[] array2)
{
    var result = array1.Length == array2.Length;

    for (var i = 0;
        i < array1.Length && i < array2.Length;
        ++i)
    {
        result &= array1[i] == array2[i];
    }

    return result;
}
```

This version of Compare has the same method signature as the previous example. First, there is a length equality check done against the length of the two-byte arrays, and this sets the result field to either True or False. Even if the result is False, the method continues to run. Next, the method iterates through the arrays and checks each element.

If any element is not equal, then the result gets set to `False`, and the method carries on testing, which means that no matter whether the arrays are identical or not, the comparison method takes the same length of time to execute and, therefore, will not leak information to an attacker.

Extending with Digital Signatures

Extending our example using HMACs for integrity gives us a lot of benefits when it comes to sending data from the sender to the receiver because we can detect if the encrypted messages have been corrupted or tampered with. By using the HMAC, we can ensure that the recipient can only recalculate the HMAC if they first recover the session key using their private key.

What we want to do now though is extend the example by incorporating non-repudiation with digital signatures. What this means is that before the sender (Alice), sends the message to the recipient (Bob), she first takes a digital signature of our HMAC using her private key. What that means for Bob is that when he receives the packet of data and verifies the digital signature, if it returns true, he is confident that Alice sent the message.

We follow through with our Alice and Bob example using the process illustrated in Figure 9-11.

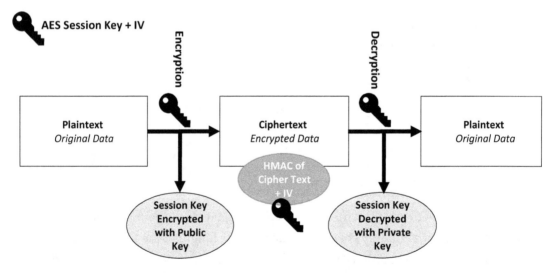

Figure 9-11. *The extended hybrid encryption process containing a digital signature*

First, **Alice** sends a message to **Bob** using hybrid encryption with built-in integrity checking and a digital signature.

Alice generates a new 256-bit (32-byte) AES session key.

Alice then generates a new 128-bit (16-byte) IV.

Alice then encrypts her message with AES using the session key and the IV.

Alice encrypts the session key with RSA and **Bob's** public key.

Alice calculates the HMAC of the encrypted data and IV combined using the un-encrypted AES session key as the key for the HMAC which means that the recipient can only recalculate the same hash once they have decrypted the AES session key with their private key.

Alice now calculates the digital signature of the HMAC, which we just created, using her private signing key.

Alice stores the encrypted data, encrypted AES session key, IV, and digital signature in a separate structure or file (see Figure 9-12), which is the packet of data that will be sent to **Bob**.

Encrypted Data Packet

RSA Encrypted Session Key
AES Initialization Vector
AES Encrypted Data
HMAC (SHA-256) of Encrypted Data
Digital Signature of HMAC

Figure 9-12. *The encrypted packet extended to contain a digital signature*

Now **Bob** has this packet of information he wants to decrypt it.

To do this, he follows the following process.

Bob decrypts the encrypted AES session key by using RSA and his private key.

Bob recalculates the HMAC of the encrypted data and IV using the decrypted AES session key.

Bob compares his HMAC to the HMAC sent with the message. If the HMAC fields match, then the data is intact, and it is safe to decrypt the message.

If the HMACs do not match, then we don't have message integrity, and the message should be discarded. Now that we have verified the HMAC, we can verify the digital signature to verify the authenticity of the message. If the HMACs match, then we know the data hasn't been corrupted or tampered with while in transit. If they don't match, then we abort the process as we do not trust the message.

The signature is then verified using **Alice's** public signing key. If the signature returns true, we have a valid digital signature. We trust that it was **Alice** who sent the original message because she needed to use her private key to sign it. If the signature verification returns false, then we do not trust the origin of the message because either the message was not signed by **Alice's** private signing key, or the data that was signed is different from what we expect.

Bob then decrypts the encrypted data by using the decrypted AES session key and the IV if the HMACS matched and the digital signature was valid.

Bob reads the decrypted message.

Let's now show this in practice in the next code demonstration.

First, we need to extend our `EncryptedPacket` class to contain a digital signature. The following code shows the completed version of `EncryptedPacket` with a new byte array for the signature.

```
public class EncryptedPacket
{
    public byte[] EncryptedSessionKey;
    public byte[] EncryptedData;
    public byte[] Iv;
    public byte[] Hmac;
    public byte[] Signature;
}
```

Our new version of the hybrid encryption scheme requires the calculation and verification of digital signatures. The following code is the class we are going to use for implementing the digital signatures. This is the same implementation that we worked through in Chapter 8. The `DigitalSignature` class contains three methods. First, the `AssignNewKey` method generates public and private key pairs, which are needed to create and verify the signatures.

Then the `SignData` method takes a byte array of a hash to create the digital signature. Digital signatures in .NET are based on RSA, which means there is a limit to the amount of data we can encrypt at a time which is why we create the signature of a hash instead. When the digital signature is created, it is returned as a byte array.

The last method is VerifySignature, which takes as parameters a byte array of the hash that we created the original signature for, and a byte array of the original digital signature. VerifySignature then checks that the signature matches the hash; if it does, VerifySignature returns true.

```
public class DigitalSignature
{
    private RSAParameters _publicKey;
    private RSAParameters _privateKey;

    public void AssignNewKey()
    {
        using (var rsa = new RSACryptoServiceProvider(2048))
        {
            rsa.PersistKeyInCsp = false;
            _publicKey = rsa.ExportParameters(false);
            _privateKey = rsa.ExportParameters(true);
        }
    }

    public byte[] SignData(byte[] hashOfDataToSign)
    {
        using (var rsa = new RSACryptoServiceProvider())
        {
            rsa.PersistKeyInCsp = false;
            rsa.ImportParameters(_privateKey);

            var rsaFormatter = new RSAPKCS1SignatureFormatter(rsa);

            rsaFormatter.SetHashAlgorithm("SHA256");

            return rsaFormatter.CreateSignature(
                                    hashOfDataToSign);
        }
    }
```

```
    public bool VerifySignature(byte[] hashOfDataToSign,
                                byte[] signature)
    {
        using (var rsa = new RSACryptoServiceProvider())
        {
            rsa.ImportParameters(_publicKey);

            var rsaDeformatter = new RSAPKCS1SignatureDeformatter(rsa);

            rsaDeformatter.SetHashAlgorithm("SHA256");

            return rsaDeformatter.VerifySignature(
                        hashOfDataToSign, signature);
        }
    }
}
```

Let's now look at extending the hybrid encryption example. The following code is identical to the previous example of hybrid encryption with integrity, apart from the code highlighted in bold.

```
private readonly AesEncryption _aes = new AesEncryption();

public EncryptedPacket EncryptData(byte[] original,
                        RSAWithRSAParameterKey rsaParams,
                        DigitalSignature digitalSignature)
{
    var sessionKey = _aes.GenerateRandomNumber(32);

    var encryptedPacket = new EncryptedPacket
      {
          Iv = _aes.GenerateRandomNumber(16)
      };

    encryptedPacket.EncryptedData = _aes.Encrypt(original, sessionKey,
                                    encryptedPacket.Iv);

    encryptedPacket.EncryptedSessionKey = rsaParams.EncryptData(sessionKey);
```

```
using (var hmac = new HMACSHA256(sessionKey))
{
    encryptedPacket.Hmac = hmac.ComputeHash(
            Combine(encryptedPacket.EncryptedData,
                    encryptedPacket.Iv));
}

encryptedPacket.Signature = digitalSignature.SignData(
                                    encryptedPacket.Hmac);

return encryptedPacket;
}
```

Once the HMAC has been calculated of the encrypted data and IV and stored in the EncryptedPacket, the final step is to create the digital signature. We create the digital signature by passing in the HMAC. This digital signature is then stored in our EncryptedPacket, ready to for the whole structure to be sent to the message recipient.

The following code shows our updated DecryptData method, which, again, is the same as the previous hybrid encryption example, except for the new section highlighted in bold.

```
public byte[] DecryptData(EncryptedPacket encryptedPacket,
                          RSAWithRSAParameterKey rsaParams,
                          DigitalSignature digitalSignature)
{
    var decryptedSessionKey = rsaParams.DecryptData(
                    encryptedPacket.EncryptedSessionKey);

    using (var hmac = new HMACSHA256(decryptedSessionKey))
    {
        var hmacToCheck = hmac.ComputeHash(
                    Combine(encryptedPacket.EncryptedData,
                    encryptedPacket.Iv));

        if (!Compare(encryptedPacket.Hmac, hmacToCheck))
        {
            throw new CryptographicException(
```

```
                    "HMAC does not match encrypted packet.");
        }
    }

    if (!digitalSignature.VerifySignature(
                        encryptedPacket.Hmac,
                        encryptedPacket.Signature))
    {
            throw new CryptographicException(
                "Digital Signature can not be verified.");
    }

    var decryptedData = _aes.Decrypt(
                        encryptedPacket.EncryptedData,
                        decryptedSessionKey,
                        encryptedPacket.Iv);

    return decryptedData;
}
```

In the update DecryptData method, as soon as we check that the HMAC for the message is valid, which indicates that the message hasn't been tampered with or corrupted in transit, we can verify the digital signature. We do this by calling VerifySignature on our digital signature implementation and provide the HMAC from our encrypted packet; we also provide the digital signature that also is stored in the EncryptedPacket. At this point, we are happy that the HMAC is valid. If VerifySignature returns true, then we can proceed to decrypt our original data with AES. If VerifySignature returns false, then we throw an exception and then abort the method.

By including the facility to store and verify a digital signature, if the signature verifies correctly, we can be sure that the sender of the message was indeed who they claim to be. Because the digital signature has to be generated using the senders private key, and we use the senders public key to enable verification of the digital signature; this gives us non-repudiation on our hybrid encryption example.

Earlier in the book, we discussed the four pillars of cryptography, confidentiality, integrity, authentication, and non-repudiation. What we built in this hybrid encryption example satisfies all four of those pillars.

Summary

In this chapter, we took a lot of what we learned so far, including random number generation, hashing and authenticated hashing, symmetric encryption with AES, asymmetric encryption with RSA, and digital signatures, and combined them to create a *hybrid encryption scheme*.

Public key cryptography systems are very convenient to use because they don't require the sender and receiver of a message to share a secret key, such as an AES symmetric key, in order to communicate securely. However, they do rely on complicated mathematics and are much more inefficient than comparable symmetric-key algorithms.

Encrypting all of your data using an asymmetric encryption system such as RSA can be very inefficient, which means it is a good idea to use a blended approach called *hybrid cryptography*. A hybrid cryptosystem uses the best of both asymmetric and symmetric cryptography.

For large pieces of data, the majority of the encryption and decryption is done by the more efficient symmetric-key scheme such as AES in our case, while the inefficient public-key scheme, RSA, is used to encrypt and decrypt our key used for AES.

Once we had a hybrid encryption system running that uses AES and RSA, we extended this concept further by adding built-in integrity checking and authentication. This took the form of using HMACs to hash the encrypted data using the unencrypted AES session key. This meant that only the recipient who controls the private key could decrypt the session key and then recalculate the hash to check if the message has been corrupted or tampered with.

Finally, we extended the hybrid encryption system by adding in non-repudiation so that we can ensure that we trusted who the sender of the original message was, as only the sender could create the digital signature using their private key.

In the next chapter, we extend our hybrid scheme further by improving how we manage our public and private keys. We do this by exploring hardware security modules using Microsoft Azure Key Vault.

CHAPTER 10

Key Storage and Azure Key Vault

In previous chapters, we built a sophisticated encryption example that had the ability to use symmetric encryption to encrypt our data while protecting the symmetric encryption keys utilizing an RSA public and private key pair. While symmetric encryption is fast and efficient, moving the keys between multiple parties is very hard to achieve safely; this is why we use RSA to encrypt the symmetric key. The key is encrypted using the recipient's public key (which can be known by anyone) and is then decrypted using the recipients private key (which only they know).

The next step in our quest for robust encryption is to now think about how we can protect the RSA encryption key. In this chapter, we are going to explore an exciting feature of Microsoft's Azure cloud computing platform called Azure Key Vault. Key Vault gives regular developers, and smaller companies access to robust key protection hardware that was traditionally only accessible to large corporations like banks and pharmaceutical companies. Azure Key Vault gives any company access to the same level of protection and using the techniques over the next few chapters; you can get the costs down very low.

Exploring Key Management Options

The example code we built up in the preceding chapters did not put any emphasis on protecting the RSA keys that were generated. For ease of use with the examples, we kept the RSA keys loaded into in-memory objects. While this was ok for the examples, we need to look at better protecting those keys. Let's explore some key management options that are available to us before I go into more detail with Azure Key Vault.

© Stephen Haunts 2019
S. Haunts, *Applied Cryptography in .NET and Azure Key Vault*,
https://doi.org/10.1007/978-1-4842-4375-6_10

143

The first option to discuss, which is a bad option, is that of storing your keys as files on the file system (see Figure 10-1), which may seem like common sense to state that this is a bad idea, but the reason I mention it here is because I have worked at two organizations that took this approach. Storing any key material in a flat file on the system is terrible because it is tough to control who has access to those files. We see time and time again in the press that files get stolen from organizations due to people having access to a file system. People external to the company may not be able to access the file system, but there is always someone in the company that can. If anyone has access to the keys, then you should consider your system compromised.

Figure 10-1. *Do not store key material in flat files on the file system*

The next key management option is certificates. The idea of using certificates to store key material has been around for a very long time. It is one of the most common ways of approaching the problem. A certificate stores information on who the certificate was issued by and who it was issued to, along with key material that is digitally signed by a root certificate issued to an organization. Signing the key material and other certificates offers a chain of trust between the issued certificate and a trusted authority.

Certificates are loaded into a certificate store directly on a server to make them available to the applications that require them. Certificates are well supported and understood by IT professionals. They need minimal to no involvement from an end user of a system as they can be preloaded as part of an installation process and they don't require any additional hardware, although certificates can be loaded into hardware certificate stores. The vast majority of enterprise systems in existence today use certificates either directly by the software they have developed, or due to a third-party system that they have integrated with; certificates are a common way of authenticating with third-party systems and APIs.

The next level of key management protection is to use a *hardware security module* (HSM), which is a hardware appliance that is directly installed into a data center for the express purpose of storing encryption keys and certificates. Typically, it is a 1u or 2u rackmount appliance that is tamper resistant, which means that if anyone tries to perform a software hack or physically penetrate the box, it wipes itself clean. It has multiple sensors that can detect if the screws are removed, or there is a change in temperature within the box. The internal chips can also be covered in resin as well as being electronically shielded to stop an attacker trying to read electric signals within the device. HSMs provide a secure and robust way to store encryption key material for enterprises, but they have one downside. They are very expensive. The costs can quickly run between tens of thousands of dollars up to and over one hundred thousand dollars. Typically, you would have at least two of these devices that are co-located in different data centers so that if one unit is compromised and it wipes itself, the other device still has access to the key material.

For a large corporation like a bank, the cost isn't so much of an issue, but for smaller companies, these costs can be prohibitive making them not be an option; which is where Microsoft Azure comes into play with their excellent Key Vault service.

Introducing Azure Key Vault

Azure Key Vault is a service provided by Microsoft as part of their Azure Cloud Computing platform that makes the functionality of HSMs available to anyone for a fraction of the cost. Even though Microsoft provides a software abstraction to the service, underneath there is real HSM hardware being used. Microsoft has put into each of its regional data centers a series of devices called the nShield by a company Thales Security, which means Microsoft has taken the financial hit on the cost of the hardware that they rent out to software developers for a minimal price. The fundamental shift between you paying for an HSM to a pay-as-you consume model has enormous implications as this means you can now take advantage of the same level of secure key management that banks have been enjoying for many years.

When you set up Azure Key Vault, which we look at in a moment, you can configure it to work in two modes, software, and hardware, which both have cost implications in their use. The one common feature between both hardware and software mode is that your encryption keys are always stored and protected on the HSM hardware. You get that no matter what configuration you use, but there are other differences between them.

Azure Key Vault Hardware Mode

When you configure Key Vault to work in hardware mode, you get the most benefit from the service because not only are keys stored in the hardware, but all operations such as encryption, decryption, and digital signatures are also performed on the device, which gives you the high level of protection when using Key Vault. The extra level of security that this affords does come at a cost as you need to use a premium service plan, but the additional cost gives you the extra protection that you would want in a production system.

Azure Key Vault Software Mode

On the flip side, when you configure Key Vault to work in software mode, your keys are stored on the hardware, but any other operations, such as encryption, decryption, and digital signatures are performed outside of the HSM hardware using standard Azure compute virtual machines. Since there is less work on the HSM, you save money. From a software interface point of view, there is no difference in how you use Key Vault between hardware and software mode; the differences are transparent to a developer.

When you are planning your testing and production environments for your software application, it is a good idea to use Key Vault in software mode for your testing environments as you can keep the costs low, and then use the hardware version for your production environment as this gives you the most significant level of protection.

Keys vs. Secrets

Azure Key Vault allows you to store three objects within the vault. The first is certificates where you can store certificates instead of a local machine key store on Windows. Then there are keys, which are stored by Key Vault. RSA keys range in length from 2048 bit to 4096 bit. You can also store secrets. Secrets are up to 25K blocks of text that are encrypted using a master key that is managed by Key Vault.

Secrets are a fantastic way of storing application secrets that you don't want to expose in configuration files or source control. Examples of such secrets might be database connection strings or any API key or authentication information for third-party services. We look at some patterns of working with secrets in the next chapter as they provide a compelling way to protect application secrets that you don't want to be exposed to third parties.

Azure Key Vault Example Costs

I mentioned that purchasing HSM hardware can cost tens of thousands of dollars, but using a service like Azure Key Vault significantly reduces that cost by letting you pay for what you use.

Let's run through some example costs to illustrate just how low the costs are. As with any cloud service, prices are liable to change, so treat these prices shown in Table 10-1 as an illustration only to see that there is a big price difference between buying the hardware and renting it on a cloud system like Azure.

When using Azure Key Vault, there are two pricing tiers: standard, and premium. The premium tier has higher cost implications when you use higher-strength RSA keys. The first set of costs are storing and retrieving secrets and certificates.

Table 10-1. *Non-Key Operations*

Service	Standard	Premium
Secret Operations	$0.03 per 10,000 operation	$0.03 per 10,000 operation
Certificate Operations	Renewals $3 per request All other operation $0.03 per 10,000	Renewals $3 per request All other operation $0.03 per 10,000

The costs between the standard and premium tiers here are the same. Secrets cost $0.03 per 10,000 operations. Certificates cost $3 for renewals and $0.03 per 10,000 read operations.

For key-based operations, pricing depends on whether you are using the software or hardware HSM. For a software HSM configuration (Table 10-2), all key operations for an RSA 2048-bit key, whether a standard or premium tier, costs $0.03 per 10,000 operations. For higher-strength RSA 3072- to 4096-bit keys, you are looking at $0.15 per 10,000 operations.

Table 10-2. *Software HSM Key Operations*

Service	Standard	Premium
RSA 2048-bit keys	$0.03 per 10,000 operations	$0.03 per 10,000 operations
RSA 3072 – 4096-bit keys	$0.15 per 10,000 operations	$0.15 per 10,000 operations

These prices are low. The software configuration is ideal for test environments. The prices start to change and go higher if you are using the full hardware configuration. For this configuration, you have to use the premium pricing tier. To use the full hardware HSM encryption operations, you are looking at $1 per key and $0.03 per 10,000 operations for an RSA 2048-bit key. If you need to use stronger keys, such as 3072- to 4096-bit RSA keys, then the costs are much higher.

The prices for the higher-strength keys are staggered, depending on how many you have. The first 250 keys are $5 per key. Keys from 251 to 1500 are $2.50 per key, and so on, as illustrated in Table 10-3. Then once you have the key, you are charged $0.15 per 10,000 encryption and decryption operations.

Table 10-3. *Hardware HSM Key Operations*

Service	Standard	Premium
RSA 2048-bit keys	N/A	$1 per Key + $0.03 per 10,000 operation
RSA 3072 – 4096-bit keys	N/A	First 250 keys = $5 per key
		251 – 1500 keys $2.50 per key
		1501 – 4000 keys £0.90 per key
		4001+ keys $0.40 per key
		+ $0.15 per 10,000 operations

As you can see, the high-strength keys with full hardware encryption and decryption are significantly more expensive, which is why it is a good idea to use this configuration for your production environment and the less expensive software configuration for your test environments.

Setting up Azure Key Vault

Before we look at how to program against Azure Key Vault, let's first look at the setup and application registration process. In the fast-moving world of cloud computing, it is possible for the installation instructions to change slightly, so in this section,

I cover how they were at the time of writing, but it is always prudent to check the latest documentation provided by Microsoft at `https://docs.microsoft.com/en-gb/azure/key-vault/key-vault-get-started`.

The best way to set up Key Vault is by using Azure PowerShell commands. You can use commands in Azure Cloud Shell, which is available in the online Azure Portal, or you can install them onto your local machine to use from the PowerShell command line. Instructions for installing and configuring the Azure PowerShell commands can be found at `https://docs.microsoft.com/en-us/powershell/azure/overview`.

Creating a Key Vault

The first step to create a Key Vault from PowerShell is to connect to your Azure Subscription. First, you need to connect to Azure using the following command.

```
Connect-AzureRmAccount
```

You are prompted to type in your Azure credentials to connect. If you have one Azure subscription linked to this account, then you are connected and ready to go. If you have multiple Azure subscriptions, then you can specify which subscription you want to use for Key Vault. To get a list of active subscriptions use the following command.

```
Get-AzureRmSubscription
```

Once you have the subscription ID, you want to connect with, use the following command to set the subscription context.

```
Set-AzureRmContext -SubscriptionId <subscription ID>
```

Once you have connected to Azure, you need to create a resource group to put Key Vault in if you don't have one set up already. To create a resource group, execute the following command.

```
New-AzureRmResourceGroup -Name 'MyResourceGroup' -Location 'East US'
```

This creates a new resource group named MyResourceGroup, which is located in the East US data center. To find the location code for your desired region, you can access the latest list from Microsoft at `https://azure.microsoft.com/en-gb/global-infrastructure/locations/`.

The next step is to create Key Vault. This is done with the `New-AzureRmKeyVault` command, where you need to specify the name of the vault, the resource group and the regional location of the Azure data center that you want to create Key Vault in.

```
New-AzureRmKeyVault -VaultName 'MyAzureVault' -ResourceGroupName
'MyResourceGroup' -Location 'East US'
```

When you execute this command, you see two important properties displayed: the vault name, which in this case is MyAzureVault, and the Vault URI, which is `https://myvault.vault.azure.net`. The vault URI is important when we connect to the vault later in this chapter.

At the moment, the vault that would have been created is on the standard pricing tier. If you want to create a vault on the premium pricing tier that supports the higher-strength RSA keys, then you need to specify the `-SKU` property when creating the vault, which means the vault creation command is as follows.

```
New-AzureRmKeyVault -VaultName 'MyAzureVault' -ResourceGroupName
'MyResourceGroup' -Location 'East US' -SKU 'Premium'
```

At this point, we could add keys and secrets to Key Vault. Before we look at this, let's first look at how to register your application to work with Key Vault.

Registering Your Application with Azure Active Directory

Now that we have looked at how to create the Azure Key Vault, we need to register our application with a token for Azure Active Directory. Once this is done, you receive two pieces of information that you need to supply your application; this is the application ID and an authentication key. Your software application needs to provide these two pieces of information to get a token to use Key Vault.

To register your application with Azure Active Directory, you need to do the following steps.

1. Sign in to the Azure Portal.

2. On the left panel, click App Registrations. If you cannot see this, click "All services", then find App Registrations.

3. Click New Application Registration.

4. On the Create blade, you need to provide a name for your application and select Web app / API from the application type drop-down menu. You also need to provide a sign-on URL for your application, such as https://www.myapplication.com. It doesn't matter if the site actually exists, you need to specify a URL. This is seen in Figure 10-2.

Figure 10-2. *Creating an app registration*

5. Click the Create button to register your application.

6. When the application is created, click your application name in the list.

7. Click the registered app blade and copy the application ID, and store it for use in your application, as seen in Figure 10-3.

Figure 10-3. *Make note of the application ID for your application*

8. Click Settings, which shows the blade, and then click Keys (see Figure 10-4).

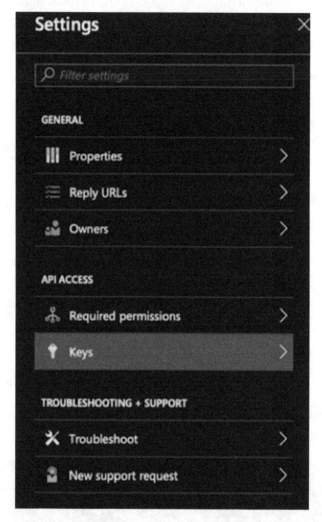

Figure 10-4. *Accessing the shared secret that you need for your application*

9. Type in the description of the application in the Key Description field, and select a duration for the authentication key. Click Save. When the page has refreshed you see a shared secret value be displayed. This shared secret expires after the elapsed duration, so this step needs to be reproduced when the shared secret expires (see Figure 10-5).

Figure 10-5. *Copy the shared secret value because you can only view it once*

10. Make a note of this shared secret value because you need to
     provide it for your application. You only have one opportunity to
     copy this value as it is not shown in the clear again.

Now that you have registered your application with Azure Active Directory and you
have access to your application ID and authentication key, you need to authorize your
application to use keys and secrets.

Authorize Your Application to Use Keys and Secrets

To authorize your application to encrypt/decrypt and sign/verify data you need a
PowerShell command called `Set-AzureRmKeyVaultAccessPolicy`. To execute this
command, you need your Key Vault name and the application ID that was created when
the application was registered with Azure Active Directory.

Let's assume they are

Key Vault Name: MyKeyVault

Application ID: 1f3dcdd-465a-56ea-75a9-3edf23ddd32dac

To enable encryption and signing permissions to your application you use the
preceding information with the following PowerShell command.

```
Set-AzureRmKeyVaultAccessPolicy -VaultName 'MyKeyVault'
-ServicePrincipalName '1f3dcdd-465a-56ea-75a9-3edf23ddd32dac'-
PermissionsToKeys decrypt,sign
```

If you want to authorize the reading of secrets in your application, you would use the following command.

```
Set-AzureRmKeyVaultAccessPolicy -VaultName 'MyKeyVault'
-ServicePrincipalName '1f3dcdd-465a-56ea-75a9-3edf23ddd32dac'-
PermissionsToSecrets Get
```

You can also set the principle and permissions for Key Vault from the Azure Portal. First, select the Key Vault resource in Azure to bring up its blade, and then click "Access policies", as seen in Figure 10-6.

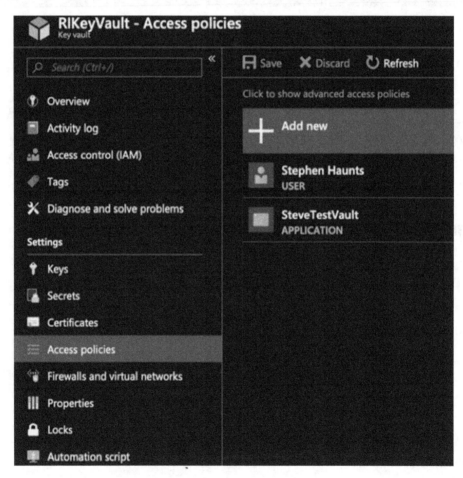

Figure 10-6. *Assign your app registration to your Key Vault access policy*

Then click "Add new", where you can set the permissions for keys, secrets, and certificates (see Figure 10-7). For testing purposes, you can select all permissions across each of these, but for production, you need to select based on your needs.

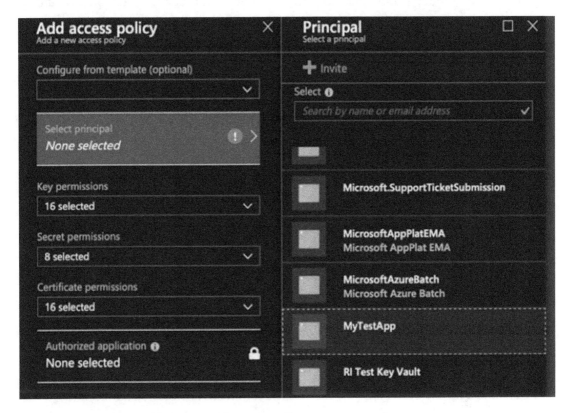

Figure 10-7. *Insert the app registration that you created*

When you have selected the key, secret, and certificate permissions, click "Select principle" and select the app registration that you created. This links that application ID and shared secret to Key Vault, so that it knows which set of authentication permissions to use. When you have done this, hit OK, and then Save. The app registration and permissions are set for your Key Vault.

Manually Creating Keys and Secrets

Now that we have looked the creation of Key Vault and registering/authorizing the application with Azure Active Directory, let's look at how to manually create keys and secrets in the vault before we explore doing this from our sample application.

Add a Software Protected Key

A software-protected key means the key is stored at rest in the actual HSM hardware, but any encryption or decryption operations that happen with that key occurs on a virtual machine outside of Key Vault. All of this happens transparently behind the scenes when you use the key, but it is an excellent way to keep your costs down, which makes the software-based key ideal for test environments.

Creating a key from PowerShell is very easy. You do it with the following command.

```
Add-AzureKeyVaultKey -VaultName 'MyKeyVault' -Name 'MyKeyName' -Destination
'Software'
```

This creates the key and gives it an ID, which is a URI. In this case, the URI for the key is `https://MyKeyVault.vault.azure.net/keys/MyKeyName`.

This retrieves the latest version of that key.

Add a Hardware-Protected Key

If you have created a Key Vault that supports hardware keys by using the SKU flag, then you can create hardware keys where encryption and decryption operations are carried out in the actual HSM hardware as opposed to a software-based virtual machine. Using these types of keys incur a higher cost as we discussed earlier, but they are an excellent option for production environments.

To create a hardware-based key, you use the following PowerShell command.

```
Add-AzureKeyVaultKey -VaultName 'MyKeyVault' -Name 'MyHSMKeyName'
-Destination 'HSM'
```

Add a Key from a PFX Certificate File

If you have an existing set of keys in a PFX certificate file, then you can load these up directly into Key Vault. A PFX file is a format called the personal information exchange format, which lets you transfer certificates and their private keys between machines. A password protects these files typically, so you first need to convert the password to a secure string. Let's assume the password is P455w0rd. To turn this to a secure string, you would run the following command.

```
$password = ConvertTo-SecureString -String 'P455w0rd' -AsPlainText -Force
```

Next, you need to run a command to load the PFX and keys into Key Vault. Assuming the PFX file is called mycert.pfx, then you would run the following command.

```
$key = Add-AzureKeyVaultKey -VaultName 'MyKeyVault' -Name 'MyImportedKey'
-KeyFilePath 'c:\mycert.pfx' -KeyFilePassword $password
```

This command loads the certificate using your converted password from the file and creates a new Key Vault key called MyImportedKey. From here, you would use the key the same as a Key Vault specifically generated key.

If you want to load a PFX file as a hardware-based key, then you would run the following commands; the first of which converts the password to a secure string.

```
$password = ConvertTo-SecureString -String 'P455w0rd' -AsPlainText -Force
```

Then you import the PFX file as a hardware key as follows with the Destination flag set to HSM.

```
$key = Add-AzureKeyVaultKey -VaultName 'MyKeyVault' -Name 'MyHSMPfxKey'
-KeyFilePath 'c:\mycert.pfx' -KeyFilePassword $password -Destination 'HSM'
```

Once this is done, the key is available to use in your application.

Add a Secret

As well as manually creating keys and importing PFX files, you can also manually add secrets to the vault from PowerShell. Secrets are up to 25K blobs of text that you can store in Key Vault. Secrets are ideal for storing configuration items that you would not want to be exposed in your source code or configuration files like database connection passwords.

The following example takes a password and again converts it into a secure.

```
$password = ConvertTo-SecureString -String 'P455w0rd' -AsPlainText -Force
```

Then we upload the text as a secret into Key Vault and give it a name, so it can be retrieved later.

```
$secret = Set-AzureKeyVaultSecret -VaultName 'MyKeyVault' -Name
'MyDatabasePassword' -SecretValue $password
```

As with keys, the secret can be accessed with a URI. When our sample application uses a secret from the vault, it uses a URI (see https://MyKeyVault.vault.azure.net/secrets/DatabasePassword).

You can also access the contents of the secret from PowerShell with the following command.

```
(get-azurekeyvaultsecret -vaultName "MyKeyVault" -name "DatabasePassword").
SecretValueText
```

Now that we have looked at the setup and application registration process with PowerShell, let's look at how to access Key Vault from C#.

Azure Key Vault "Hello World" Application

Before we look at some specific usage patterns around using Azure Key Vault, let's first try a Hello World style application that creates a key in the vault and then perform a simple encrypt and decrypt operation with that key. If you have the sample code for this book, then we are going to be using the SimpleEncryptDecrypt project.

To use the Azure Key Vault client library in your .NET Core or .NET Framework project, you first need to add the Microsoft.Azure.KeyVault NuGet package, as you can see in Figure 10-8.

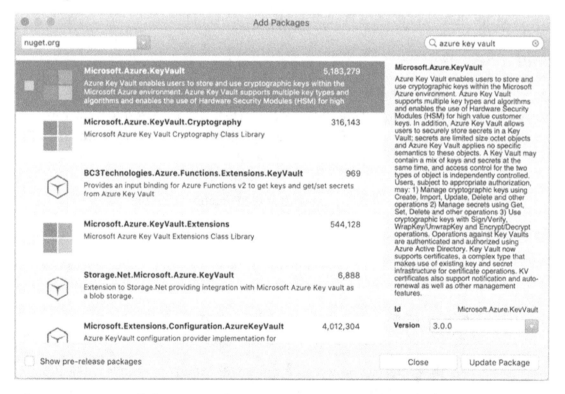

Figure 10-8. *Install the Microsoft.Azure.KeyVault NuGet package*

The package loads any dependencies that are needed to access Key Vault programmatically. The client library abstracts away the HTTP interface that is used to talk to Key Vault giving developers an easy-to-use programming interface. For the remainder of the book, there is a specific list of operations that we are required to use from the client library.

- Creating and deleting encryption keys

- Encrypting and decrypting with RSA

- Getting and setting secrets

- Creating and verifying digital signatures

To make working with this subset of features more manageable, the example first creates an interface called IKeyVault where we define the interface of the operations we require.

```
public interface IKeyVault
{
    Task<string> CreateKeyAsync(string keyName);
    Task DeleteKeyAsync(string keyName);

    Task<byte[]> EncryptAsync(string keyId, byte[] dataToEncrypt);

    Task<byte[]> DecryptAsync(string keyId, byte[] dataToDecrypt);

    Task<string> SetSecretAsync(string secretName, string secretValue);

    Task<string> GetSecretAsync(string secretName);

    Task<byte[]> Sign(string keyId, byte[] hash);

    Task<bool> Verify(string keyId, byte[] hash, byte[] signature);
}
```

Next, in the sample project, there is a helper function base class called KeyVaultBase. The KeyVaultBase class contains helper methods needed by the rest of the application, which includes a helper method called GetKeyUri, which retrieves the URI for a named key from the vault, GetKeyBundle that contains key properties and attributes, and GetAccessTokenAsync for handling the access token for accessing Key Vault.

```
using using Microsoft.Azure.KeyVault;
using Microsoft.Azure.KeyVault.Models;
using Microsoft.Azure.KeyVault.WebKey;

public class KeyVaultBase
{
    protected KeyVaultClient KeyVaultClient;
    protected ClientCredential ClientCredential;
    protected string VaultAddress;

    protected string GetKeyUri(string keyName)
    {
        var retrievedKey = KeyVaultClient.GetKeyAsync(
                            VaultAddress, keyName)
                            .GetAwaiter().GetResult();

        return retrievedKey.Key.Kid;
    }

    protected KeyBundle GetKeyBundle()
    {
        var defaultKeyBundle = new KeyBundle
        {
            Key = new JsonWebKey
            {
                Kty = JsonWebKeyType.Rsa
            },
            Attributes = new KeyAttributes
            {
                Enabled = true,
                Expires = DateTime.Now.AddYears(1)
            }
        };
```

```
        return defaultKeyBundle;
    }

    protected Dictionary<string, string> GetKeyTags()
    {
        return new Dictionary<string, string>
        {
           { "purpose", "Master Key" },
           { "MyApp Core", "MyApp" }
        };
    }

    protected Dictionary<string, string> GetSecretTags()
    {
        return new Dictionary<string, string>
        {
           { "purpose", "Encrypted Secret" },
             { "MyApp Core", "MyApp" } };
      }

    protected async Task<string> GetAccessTokenAsync(string authority,
                                        string resource,
                                        string scope)
    {
        var context = new AuthenticationContext(
                    authority, TokenCache.DefaultShared);

        var result = await context.AcquireTokenAsync(
                          resource, ClientCredential);

        return result.AccessToken;
    }
}
```

Then a class called KeyVault is defined. It contains abstractions for the functionality that we need from the Azure Key Vault client library. The KeyVault class is the only class that our examples use. They do not use the Azure KeyVault client library directly, as illustrated in Figure 10-9.

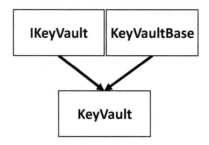

Figure 10-9. *Class hierarchy for the Key Vault helper code*

The KeyVault class contains constructor methods to create a connection to Key Vault either by using pre-baked in connection information or specified as parameters. The clientId and clientSecret are the information you should have made a note of when you registered your application for Key Vault with Azure Active Directory earlier in this chapter. The VaultAddress parameter is the URI that you can access from the Key Vault resource in the Azure Portal.

```
public KeyVault()
{
    var clientId = "your saved clientId";
    var clientSecret = "your client secret";
    VaultAddress = "the adress of your vault, i.e.
                    https://mytestvault.vault.azure.net/";

    ClientCredential = new ClientCredential(clientId, clientSecret);

    KeyVaultClient = new KeyVaultClient(
            GetAccessTokenAsync, new HttpClient());
}
public KeyVault(string clientId, string clientSecret, string vaultAddress )
{
    VaultAddress = vaultAddress;

    ClientCredential = new ClientCredential(clientId, clientSecret);

    KeyVaultClient = new KeyVaultClient(
            GetAccessTokenAsync, new HttpClient());
}
```

The next methods that are available are for creating and deleting keys within Key Vault. The `CreateKeyAsync` method works by taking a key name as a string and the makes a request to Key Vault to create the key with the specified name. When the key is generated, the key's URI from the vault is returned to the calling method. The next method exposed in this example is `DeleteKeyAsync`, and this method removes a key from Key Vault for a specified name. This is included in the example because each of the examples from this chapter and Chapter 11 cleans up after itself when it completes running by deleting its keys, but in a production application, you probably do not want to include a method for this to avoid accidental key deletion.

```
public async Task<string> CreateKeyAsync(string keyName)
{
    var keyBundle = GetKeyBundle();
    var createdKey = await KeyVaultClient.CreateKeyAsync(
                        VaultAddress, keyName,
                        keyBundle.Key.Kty,
                        keyAttributes: keyBundle.Attributes,
                        tags: GetKeyTags());

    return createdKey.KeyIdentifier.Identifier;
}

public async Task DeleteKeyAsync(string keyName)
{
    await KeyVaultClient.DeleteKeyAsync(VaultAddress, keyName);
}
```

Next, the `EncryptAsync` method that takes a `keyId`, which is the keys URI from Key Vault, and a parameter called `dataToEncrypt`, which is a byte array of some data to encrypt. An RSA encryption operation happens in Key Vault. The `DecryptAsync` method takes a `keyId` for the key to use for decryption, and a byte array called `dataToDecrypt` containing the data that needs decrypting.

```
public async Task<byte[]> EncryptAsync(
                        string keyId, byte[] dataToEncrypt)
{
    var operationResult = await KeyVaultClient.EncryptAsync(
                        keyId,
```

```
                        JsonWebKeyEncryptionAlgorithm.RSAOAEP,
                        dataToEncrypt);

    return operationResult.Result;
}

public async Task<byte[]> DecryptAsync(
                    string keyId, byte[] dataToDecrypt)
{
    var operationResult = await KeyVaultClient.DecryptAsync(
                        keyId,
                        JsonWebKeyEncryptionAlgorithm.RSAOAEP,
                        dataToDecrypt);

    return operationResult.Result;
}
```

Next, there are two methods for setting and retrieving secrets. We cover some patterns for using secrets more in the next chapter. A good way to think of secrets in Key Vault is that they are like key-value pairs that are stored in Key Vault. More like an ultra secure key-value pair NoSQL database. First, the SetSecretAsync method creates a secret by providing it with a secretName, and the actual value you want to store is passed in as secretValue. The GetSecretAsync method takes the secretName that you used when the secret was created, queries Key Vault, and returns the secret value that was stored.

```
public async Task<string> SetSecretAsync(
                        string secretName, string secretValue)
{
    var bundle = await KeyVaultClient.SetSecretAsync(
                    VaultAddress,
                    secretName,
                    secretValue,
                    null,
                    "plaintext");

    return bundle.Id;
}
```

```
public async Task<string> GetSecretAsync(string secretName)
{
    try
    {
        var bundle = await KeyVaultClient.GetSecretAsync(
                            VaultAddress, secretName);

        return bundle.Value;
    }
    catch (KeyVaultErrorException)
    {
        return string.Empty;
    }
}
```

Finally, there are two methods that are used for creating and verifying digital signatures. The first is Sign, which takes a reference to a keyId to use for generating a digital signature, which uses the stored private key. The second parameter, hash, is a byte array of a hash for the data we want to create the signature against. Remember back to when we discussed digital signatures earlier in the book. You hash the data you want to create the signature for because there are length limits on the amount of data you can use with RSA and RSA based digital signatures. The Sign method returns a byte array containing the digital signature.

The second method is called Verify, and this method takes as a parameter a keyId, which references a public key in Key Vault. The second parameter, called hash, is a byte array of the hash for some data you want to verify the signature for, and the final parameter, called signature, is the hash of the digital signature that was returned by the Sign method. The verify method returns true if the signature is correct for the hash or false otherwise if the signature does not match.

```
public async Task<byte[]> Sign(string keyId, byte[] hash)
{
    var bundle = await KeyVaultClient.SignAsync(
                        keyId, "RS256", hash);

    return bundle.Result;
}
```

```
public async Task<bool> Verify(string keyId,
                               byte[] hash,
                               byte[] signature)
{
    var result = await KeyVaultClient.VerifyAsync(
                    keyId, "RS256", hash, signature);

    return result;
}
```

The IKeyVault, KeyVaultBase, and KeyVault files are the main helper objects that we need for the rest of this example and the following examples we walk through in the next chapter. Let's now look at using these helpers to create a simple example that perform the following steps.

- Create a named RSA key in Key Vault

- Encrypt some data with that key

- Decrypt the data with the same key

- Delete the original key from Key Vault.

```
class Program
{
    static void Main(string[] args)
    {
        KeyVault().GetAwaiter().GetResult();
    }

    public static async Task KeyVault()
    {
        IKeyVault vault = new KeyVault();

        const string MY_KEY_NAME = "MyKeyVaultKey";

        string keyId = await vault.CreateKeyAsync(MY_KEY_NAME);

        Console.WriteLine("Key Written : " + keyId);
```

```
// Test encryption and decryption.
string dataToEncrypt = "Hello World!!";

byte[] encrypted = await vault.EncryptAsync(
        keyId,
        Encoding.ASCII.GetBytes(dataToEncrypt));

byte[] decrypted = await vault.DecryptAsync(
        keyId, encrypted);

var encryptedText = Convert.ToBase64String(encrypted);

var decryptedData = Encoding.UTF8.GetString(decrypted);

Console.WriteLine(
        "Encrypted Data : " + encryptedText);
Console.WriteLine(
        "Decrypted Data : " + decryptedData);

// Remove HSM backed key
await vault.DeleteKeyAsync(MY_KEY_NAME);
Console.WriteLine("Key Deleted : " + keyId);
    }
}
```

First, a key is created called MyKeyVaultKey, and the resulting URI is stored in a
variable called keyId. Then using that keyId, we encrypt a simple Hello World!! string
and store the results in a byte array. We then decrypt that data straight away using the
same keyId.

The encrypted and decrypted results are then displayed in the terminal window
before the original key is deleted. You can see the results of running this simple
application in Figure 10-10.

Figure 10-10. *Output from Key Vault–based encryption and decryption example*

The example we walked through represents a simple encryption and decryption operation using Azure Key Vault. We explore some more coding and operational patterns of using Key Vault in the next chapter.

Summary

In this chapter, we looked at Microsoft Azure Key Vault cloud computing platform. Key Vault is a software abstraction on top of traditional HSM hardware. Until services like Azure Key Vault existed, HSMs were too expensive for most, except large institutions like banks and insurance companies. With a service like Azure Key Vault, the cost of using robust key management hardware has been dramatically slashed and moved within the reach of anyone who wants to use it. The ramifications of this are massive as it means any company has the option to use HSMs to store their keys. In the next chapter, we look at some more code and usage patterns for Microsoft Azure Key Vault.

CHAPTER 11

Azure Key Vault Usage Patterns

In the preceding chapters, we built a sophisticated encryption example with the ability to encrypt data with the efficiency of AES, and uses RSA to make it easier to swap encryption keys with other users. We then looked at how to leverage and set up Azure Key Vault, which offers a cost-effective way to use a hardware security module that traditionally is out of reach to most companies, except large organizations like banks.

In this chapter, we explore some Azure Key Vault usage patterns to get the most out of the service and to keep the running costs as low as possible. I talk about the following patterns:

- Multiple environments

- Configuration as secrets

- Local key wrapping

- Password protection

- Digital signing

Once we have discussed these patterns, we upgrade the hybrid encryption example from the previous chapters to support the use of Azure Key Vault.

Multiple Environments

First, we will look at using Azure Key Vault across your software development environments. With modern software development, it is common to use numerous testing environments to help guide your software solutions through testing and into production. These environments may either be manually created environments that are nurtured

© Stephen Haunts 2019
S. Haunts, *Applied Cryptography in .NET and Azure Key Vault*,
https://doi.org/10.1007/978-1-4842-4375-6_11

through a project or scripted environments that can be rebuilt at the click of a button. It is not the purpose of this book to discuss the merits or pitfalls of either direction, but we want to look at where Azure Key Vault fits into this specifically. Let's first start with a configuration that you want to avoid, and that is to use the same Key Vault instance across all of your environments including your testing environments and productions (see Figure 11-1); this is a very bad scenario because it means you are using the same encryption keys from production across your test environments. This might be seen as a benefit if you replicate data from your production databases to test environments as it means you can then read your production data in a test environment, but this is not a good idea.

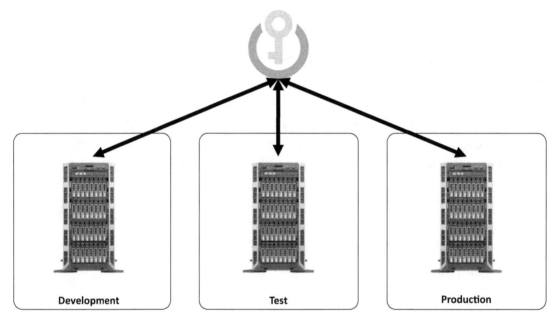

Figure 11-1. *Do not share key vault instances between test and production environments*

The benefit of using a service like Azure Key Vault is that you are trying to protect your data from potential data breaches and leaks outside your organization. If you are copying data from production to your test environments, and then using the same Key Vault instance and keys to access that data from your test environment; then you are leaving your data open for a potential data breach if a member of your organization wants to exfiltrate that data. They effectively have a copy of all the data and a way to decrypt that data with Key Vault, which is a terrible situation to be in. Don't just think that by using Key Vault you are protected from external threats who want to steal your data; it can happen from within your organization too.

If you work in an organization that reuses their environments for each project and doesn't rebuild them from scripts every time, then you may decide to build two Key Vault instances: one that is shared by the test environments and another that is used exclusively by production (see Figure 11-2). In this configuration, you use different keys between test and production, which means that you cannot copy data from production back into your test environments. This should be seen as a benefit. It could be seen as a downside because you cannot use production data for testing, which may be inconvenient but is actually a huge security risk.

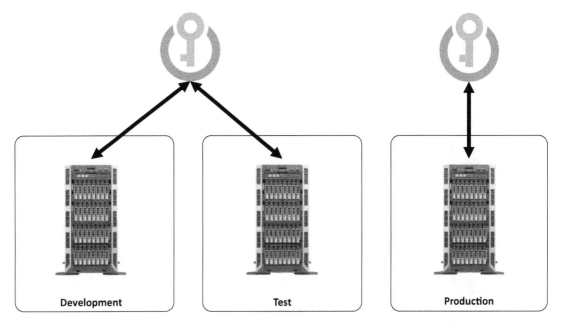

Figure 11-2. *Use a separate instance of Key Vault for production systems*

If you work in an organization that deals with financial data like credit card numbers, or you are storing personal information of individuals, then it is especially important that you protect this data to the best of your abilities, and that means making sure software development staff can't read or access that data. If you store European citizens' information, then you fall under the jurisdiction of the GDPR legislation, which can have substantial financial and reputational implications on your organization if any of the data is leaked.

By using a separate Key Vault instance for production, you can at least guarantee a level of insulation from your valuable production data. But what can you do about test data if you can't copy and read encrypted production data? In this scenario, you need to investigate ways of generating test data to seed your system, which then gives you the ability to routinely clear down your databases and then create test data to a known point.

If you need to replicate a bug from production, you can then try to replicate the data in question within your test data generator as a way of building repeatable test cases. You could even investigate a way to copy your production data to your test environment, but then have a script or process that replaces all the encrypted data like credit cards or personal data with dummy data, so you have the benefit of real production data but with the sensitive data replaced with generated test data.

If you work in an environment where you have scripted the creation of your test environments, then you are in an even better position because you can develop PowerShell scripts to create a new Key Vault instance and register a new application in Azure Active Directory for each test environment (see Figure 11-3). This gives the best situation. And coupled with a way to generate test data or anonymize production data, you have unique and reproducible environments with customer data that doesn't contain any production data protected with your production Key Vault.

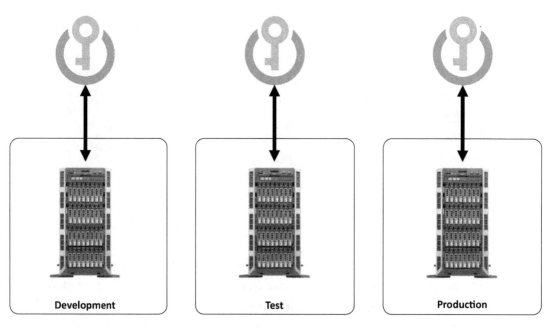

Figure 11-3. *Separate instances of Key Vault can be scripted across each environment*

If you want to keep your costs down, then you can use software based Key Vaults in your test environments where encryption and decryption operations are performed on software virtual machines within Key Vault service. For your production environment, you can use the full hardware configured version of Key vault, which incurs a higher cost, but it is a justifiable cost for your production environment. In either case, regardless of whether you use a hardware or software configured Key Vault, your keys are always stored on the hardware security module, and once those keys are in the vault, they can never come out again giving you excellent protection.

Configuration as Secrets

Azure Key Vault allows you the ability to store secrets in the Key Vault as well as manage encryption keys. Secrets are named blobs of text that can be stored up to 25K in size. The encryption of secrets in Key Vault is handled by keys managed by Microsoft, which means you do not need to worry about the key management aspect for storing and retrieving secrets. Although you do not perform the key management, Microsoft can't read what you store in your secrets.

An excellent way to think about the storage of secrets is that it is like a key-value pair NoSQL data store. You store your secret, which is the value and you give it a name that you provide when you save the value and then retrieve it again.

If you store a secret with the same identifying name each time, then a version history is maintained in Key Vault of the existing secrets. This is great if you want to keep a version history of your secrets. When a secret is added to the vault, you are given information back about URI for the secret. If you then request the secret from the vault using this URI, you are given the latest version of the secret unless you provide a version number of the desired secret.

The ideal scenario for using secrets with the Key Vault is to store anything that you do not wish an end user to see in your code, configuration files, or databases. An excellent example for this would be database connection strings, especially for production databases. Typically, the management of these connection strings has been difficult and clumsy to manage, but to store them as secrets in Key Vault turns this into a trivial problem, as you will see in the following code sample.

Another example of something you may want to store as secrets are API keys for third-party systems or even API keys that you manage for your application. By storing them in Key Vault, you can be comfortable in the knowledge that they are encrypted and protected.

Let's look at how to store and retrieve secrets using the example code framework we discussed in Chapter 10. In the following example, we have an `async` method called `KeyVault` that uses the sample framework we introduced in Chapter 10. The example starts by first creating an instance of the KeyVault class that establishes a connection to Key Vault. Remember, that in the KeyVault.cs class, we have our connection information to the vault that consists of the client ID and the client secret as well as the vault address to connect to. For the example code, you either need to insert your information in this file or use the overloaded constructor that lets you supply them separately.

```
class Program
{
    public static async Task Main(string[] args)
    {
        await KeyVault();
    }

    public static async Task KeyVault()
    {
        IKeyVault vault = new KeyVault();

        const string MY_SECRET = "MySecret";

        await vault.SetSecretAsync(MY_SECRET,
                            "Mary had a little lamb.");

        Console.WriteLine("Secret Written :" +
                        "Mary had a little lamb");

        string secret = await vault.GetSecretAsync(MY_SECRET);

        Console.WriteLine("Secret Retrieved : " + secret);
    }
}
```

Once the connection to Key Vault has been established, we define a const string that contains the name of our secret. It is the name that references the secret once it is in the vault. Next, a secret is written into the Vault by calling SetSecretAsync, which calls a method of the same name on the .NET Client library. When calling SetSecretAsync you provide the secret name you want to refer to it by, and the actual secret itself as a string, "Mary had a little lamb," in our example.

To retrieve the secret from Key Vault, you call the GetSecretAsync method and provide the name of the secret; this extracts our secret text, "Mary had a little lamb," from Key Vault. When you run the example, you see something like what's shown in Figure 11-4 in your terminal/console window.

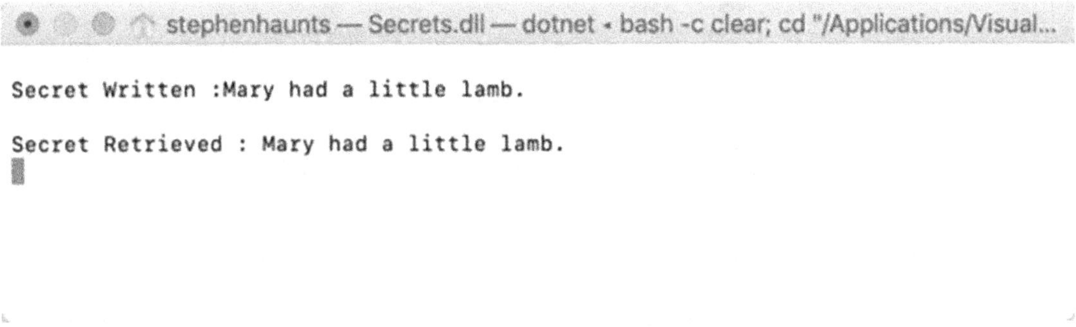

Figure 11-4. Reading and writing a secret key

On the face of it, this is a straightforward feature to allow you to store a text object by name, and it is, but this simple feature is compelling in that you can store secret configuration items securely. We see this as another example later in the chapter when looking at passwords.

Local Key Wrapping

In Chapter 10, we looked at the costs of using Key Vault, which is broadly charged based on a block of 10,000 operations. While this doesn't seem like a lot, if you are running a high scale application, those costs soon start to mount up, even though they should be significantly less than the cost of owning your own HSM hardware. Another thing to bear in mind is that the encryption and decryption operations performed by Key Vault are RSA encryption operations, which means they are slow compared to using an algorithm like AES.

What we want to do then to reduce the cost and increase the performance is to use a hybrid encryption scheme similar to what we discussed in Chapter 9. We used RSA as a way to encrypt a local AES key using our recipient's public key (see Figure 11-5). We would then encrypt our data with AES as it is faster than RSA. We could then safely send the encrypted AES key and our encrypted data to our recipient, and they would use their private RSA key to recover the AES key, which would then be used to recover the AES encrypted data.

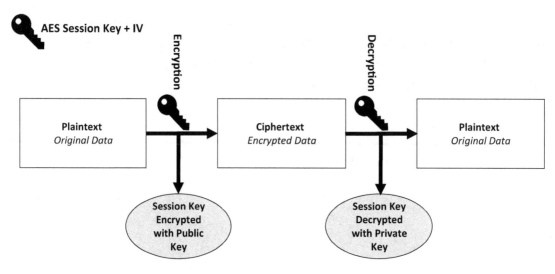

Figure 11-5. *Local key wrapping*

Using this technique means that we have the better performance of an algorithm like AES for bulk encrypting our data and the key sharing benefits of RSA. We can use the same technique by using keys managed by Key Vault. When we encrypt the local AES Key, we do it using an RSA operation and the key stored on Key Vault. When the AES key has been encrypted using Key Vault, that key can either be stored as a secret on Key Vault or stored in your database. It is ok to store the key in this state as it has already been encrypted first using Key Vault, and while this is not entirely risk free, if that encrypted key is leaked in a data breach, someone would need to be in your network with access to Key Vault to decrypt it first. When I have used this key wrapping technique before with Key Vault, I have stored the encrypted AES key as a secret in Key Vault and kept it completely away from an application database.

As well as providing the key wrapping benefits we just discussed, this technique also helps us to reduce the number of operations against Key Vault and therefore the cost of running Key Vault. Instead of calling into Key Vault each time you want to encrypt or decrypt some data, alternatively, at the start of a session (which might be a ASP.NET controller or a Web API method, for example) you would first decrypt your local AES keys at the beginning of the session and then use that decrypted key for the remainder of that session. This means those subsequent encryption/decryption operations using the decrypted AES key would not be using Key Vault at all, and therefore not incurring any cost as you are caching the decrypted AES key in local memory.

How long you chose to cache that key in-memory is an application design decision that you and your security architects need to make, but there is a balance in the tradeoff between the length of time you chose to keep that key in-memory vs. another hop out to Key Vault. Calling Key Vault doesn't just incur a financial cost but also a performance penalty. The round trip to perform a cryptographic operation with Key Vault is quite slow, so this needs to be thought about when you are architecting your application.

Let's now look at an example of using this technique to wrap a local AES key.

This example reintroduces some of the helper functions that we used earlier in the book. The first is our secure random number generator method called GenerateRandomNumber.

```
public class SecureRandom
{
    public static byte[] GenerateRandomNumber(int length)
    {
        using (var randomNumberGenerator = new RNGCryptoServiceProvider())
        {
            var randomNumber = new byte[length];
            randomNumberGenerator.GetBytes(randomNumber);

            return randomNumber;
        }
    }
}
```

This helper method generates our local AES key that we encrypt with Key Vault. The method takes an integer that indicates the length of the random number byte array that we want to be generated. The random byte array is returned from the method. We discussed secure random number generation using RNGCryptoServiceProvider in Chapter 3. The next helper class used in this example is for performing local AES encryption. The first helper method in this class is Encrypt that takes a byte array of the data that we want to encrypt, a byte array of our key and a byte array for our initialization vector. The Encrypt method uses the AesCryptoServiceProvider class in .NET to encrypt our data and return the encrypted result as a byte array.

```
public class AesEncryption
{
    public static byte[] Encrypt(byte[] dataToEncrypt,
                                 byte[] key, byte[] iv)
    {
        using (var aes = new AesCryptoServiceProvider())
        {
            aes.Mode = CipherMode.CBC;
            aes.Padding = PaddingMode.PKCS7;

            aes.Key = key;
            aes.IV = iv;

            using (var memoryStream = new MemoryStream())
            {
                var cryptoStream = new CryptoStream(
                        memoryStream, aes.CreateEncryptor(),
                        CryptoStreamMode.Write);

                cryptoStream.Write(dataToEncrypt, 0, dataToEncrypt.Length);
                cryptoStream.FlushFinalBlock();

                return memoryStream.ToArray();
            }
        }
    }

    public static byte[] Decrypt(byte[] dataToDecrypt, byte[] key, byte[] iv)

    {
        using (var aes = new AesCryptoServiceProvider())
        {
            aes.Mode = CipherMode.CBC;
            aes.Padding = PaddingMode.PKCS7;

            aes.Key = key;
            aes.IV = iv;
```

```
using (var memoryStream = new MemoryStream())
{
    var cryptoStream = new CryptoStream(
        memoryStream,
        aes.CreateDecryptor(),
        CryptoStreamMode.Write);

    cryptoStream.Write(dataToDecrypt, 0,
                        dataToDecrypt.Length);
    cryptoStream.FlushFinalBlock();

    var decryptBytes = memoryStream.ToArray();

    return decryptBytes;
}
    }
  }
}
```

The second helper method is Decrypt that takes a byte array containing our encrypted data, a byte array of the encryption key and the 16-byte initialization vector. Then using AesCryptoServiceProvider, the data is decrypted and returned as a byte array to the caller. For more information on symmetric encryption and AES, in particular, you can refer to Chapter 6.

Using these helper classes and the example Key Vault framework introduced in Chapter 10, let's hook them all up to demonstrate local key wrapping using Key Vault.

```
class Program
{
    public static async Task Main(string[] args)
    {
        await KeyVault();
    }

    public static async Task KeyVault()
    {
        IKeyVault vault = new KeyVault();

        const string MY_KEY_NAME = "StephenHauntsKey";
```

```
        string keyId = await vault.CreateKeyAsync(MY_KEY_NAME);

        byte[] localKey = SecureRandom.GenerateRandomNumber(32);

        byte[] encryptedKey = await vault.EncryptAsync(keyId, localKey);

        byte[] decryptedKey = await vault.DecryptAsync(keyId, encryptedKey);

        byte[] iv = SecureRandom.GenerateRandomNumber(16);
        byte[] encryptedData = AesEncryption.Encrypt(
            Encoding.ASCII.GetBytes("MEGA TOP SECRET STUFF"),
            decryptedKey, iv);

        byte[] decryptedMessage = AesEncryption.Decrypt(
            encryptedData,
            decryptedKey, iv);

        var encryptedText = Convert.ToBase64String(encryptedData);
        var decryptedData = Encoding.UTF8.GetString(decryptedMessage);

        await vault.DeleteKeyAsync(MY_KEY_NAME);
        Console.WriteLine("Key Deleted : " + keyId);
    }
}
```

There is quite a bit more going on here, so let's unpack this example bit by bit to see what's going on.

```
IKeyVault vault = new KeyVault();

const string MY_KEY_NAME = "MyKey";

string keyId =
    await vault.CreateKeyAsync(MY_KEY_NAME);
```

First, we want to create an instance of the KeyVault class to establish a connection to the vault. Then we define a const string called MY_KEY_NAME, which we set to be the name of our key. Then, we create the key in the vault by called CreateKeyAsync in our sample framework.

```
byte[] localKey = SecureRandom.GenerateRandomNumber(32);

byte[] encryptedKey = await vault.EncryptAsync(keyId, localKey);
```

Once we have created our Key Vault key, we then generate our local AES key using the GenerateRandomNumber help method in the SecureRandom class. This creates our local key, which is a 32-byte (256 bits) key. The next step is to encrypt this local key, and then use Key Vault by calling EncryptAsync on the KeyVault instance, providing the key ID for our newly created key on the vault. EncryptAsync returns our encrypted AES key as a byte array. At this point, you could convert it to a base64 string and store it in your database if required; which is ok to do as the key has been encrypted by Key Vault, so it is only of use to anyone if they can access Key Vault to decrypt it.

Next, we want to use the encrypted AES key to encrypt and decrypt some data locally. First, we need to decrypt that key using Key Vault.

```
byte[] decryptedKey = await vault.DecryptAsync(keyId, encryptedKey);

byte[] iv = SecureRandom.GenerateRandomNumber(16);

byte[] encryptedData = AesEncryption.Encrypt(
    Encoding.ASCII.GetBytes("MEGA TOP SECRET STUFF"),
    decryptedKey, iv);

byte[] decryptedMessage = AesEncryption.Decrypt(encryptedData,
  decryptedKey, iv);
```

First, we need to decrypt our AES key, and this is done by calling DecryptAsync on the KeyVault class by providing the encrypted key as a byte array and the key ID that was generated earlier in the example. Once the key has been decrypted, we have our raw AES key back. Then the 16-byte initialization vector is generated using the GenerateRandomNumber help method. Next, we can encrypt, and decrypt data as required as long as the decrypted AES key and initialization vector are in-memory. You need to store the initialization vector, because you will need it in the future to decrypt the data.

Exploring Key Wrapping Further

Now that we have looked at how to implement local key wrapping using Key Vault let's look at a real-world use case to help inspire the usage of this technique. Let's assume we have an online insurance claims management system that is a software as a service (SaaS) solution. This service is a white-labeled multitenant platform that is sold to insurance companies, where they can rebrand the system to fit their corporate style for their employees and portray their visual brand to their customers, the insurance claimants.

For this example, the platform is deployed into a cloud provider and acts as a single system where the data is stored, which means that the data for each insurer is stored in the same database, although the insurer has the option to pay for a separate database instance if required. With most of the data from multiple insurance companies stored together, the system partitions the data by encrypting the important *personally identifiable information* (PII) with separate master keys in the database. The insurer is issued their master key when they are onboarded into the platform. The master key is a set of keys created in Key Vault, created using the same techniques as we have discussed so far.

The master key encrypts a separate AES session key, which is stored in the database. This encrypted key encrypts all the insurers' valuable information; that is, PII data. This means that should the data from the database get breached somehow and leaked, then the data is not very useful to anyone as the data that relates to a person is encrypted using an already encrypted AES key that is protected with a key in Key Vault.

If we relate this to the diagram in Figure 11-6, you can see the SaaS platform itself in the Claims Platform box consisting of a SQL and CosmosDB database, some app services, and Key Vault. Then we have four insurers who are onboarded onto the system, which each have a set of keys created on Key Vault. These individual keys encrypt an AES session key that is stored in the database, which you can see in the table at the bottom of the diagram. The encrypted AES keys are stored along with a tenant ID, that uniquely identifies the insurance company, and the key ID, which is the key ID that is returned when the key is created in Key Vault.

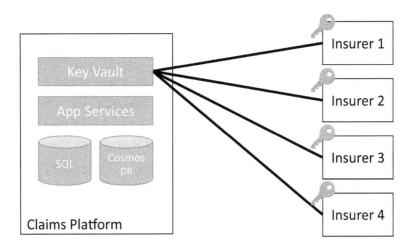

Tenant Id	Key Id	Encrypted AES Session Key
1	1	38r7289j5n79840n58v40m580v4043n85v0=
2	2	Hdkjfrwi5yuioweurowveirunvowiortvno98v=
3	3	kjdfngkdfmuto8wenrowven75ownro8ownr=
4	4	No3874n85748r898908wtirhgiwmc8wun9t=

Figure 11-6. *Issuing Key Vault keys to multiple tenants*

By storing the encrypted AES key along with the Tenant ID and Key ID, it means when an insurance company or one of their customers authenticates with the SaaS system, the correct tenant can be identified, which retrieves the key ID for that tenant's Key Vault key. The Key Vault then decrypts the encrypted AES key using the Key ID, which is stored in-memory for that session. Any encryption and decryption operations that happen in that session, all happen locally without any further hops to Key Vault, which drastically improves the performance as the encryption operations are local, so no latency is occurred over the network talking to Key Vault. Also, the cost of using Key Vault is reduced as we are only performing one operation to decrypt the local AES key.

Key Rotation and Versioning

There is another useful benefit to wrapping keys locally like this, in that it makes key rotation quite easy to do. It is good practice to change the keys in Key Vault from time to time. The cadence for this is something that should be a part of your company security policy, but none the less, having a process for rotating keys is going to be highly beneficial, and the key wrapping technique makes it easier. Let's for a minute imagine that we are not using the key wrapping technique and we are encrypting all of our PII data in the database by making requests to Key Vault to do the encryption for each field.

As we discussed, this adds a lot of network latency, but it also introduces another problem. Let's say you have 10,000 rows of information encrypted in your database using a key in Key Vault, and then your security policy dictates that you have to change that key to a new key. That in its self is easy to do, but you now have a problem in that you can no longer decrypt the data as the key has changed. You could technically get around this by storing historical Key Id's for your old keys and then in your database keep track of what data is encrypted with which key, but this adds a lot of extra complexity in your implementation.

The local key wrapping technique that we have described makes this an easy problem to solve because the only piece of data that is directly encrypted using the RSA key in Key Vault is your encrypted AES key that you have stored in the database; the rest of your data is encrypted using the decrypted AES key. Therefore, if you want to change the RSA key in Key Vault, you need to perform the following steps.

- Decrypt the AES key using the RSA key you want to replace in Key Vault.

- Create a new Key in Key Vault.

- Re-encrypt the AES key using the new RSA key and store it in the database.

- Store the key ID of the new key along with the encrypted AES key.

If you are re-creating a key in Key Vault with the same name, then Key Vault still maintains a history of old keys, which you can use by specifying the version number along with the key ID. This is useful because if anything goes wrong with the key rotating process, you still have access to the old key that encrypts the local AES key.

What we have just described is just one example of where local key wrapping could be used, but it gives a good indication to a real-world use case.

Password Protection

In Chapter 5, we spent some time looking at different password hashing and storage mechanisms. Let's review the worst solution to the best solution available in .NET.

The first and the worst solution is to store passwords as plaintext in a database. Doing this offers no protection if your database tables are leaked in a data breach. Sadly, there are still a lot of old websites out there that do use this plaintext technique, but for a new system under your control, you should never do this.

The next technique that we looked at in Chapter 5, which is better than plaintext passwords, was basic hashing of passwords. A hash is a one-way function where once a password has been hashed you shouldn't be able to go back the other way to recover the password. This principle works in theory, but hashed passwords are relatively easy to recover by performing either a brute-force attack or a rainbow table/dictionary attack. Many people still use simple passwords that might be a spouse's name or a pet name, for example, and these are very susceptible to attack. If you use a much longer and complex passphrase you are afforded a little more protection, but not by much. Modern password cracking tools like Hashcat are designed to use the powerful graphics processing units (GPUs) built into modern graphics cards. These GPU cards allow tools like Hashcat to perform billions of hashing operations per second and as these graphics' cards get more powerful each year, standard hashed passwords get easier to crack.

To try and remedy the ease of cracking hashed passwords the next technique builds on hashing by the inclusion of a salt to the password before hashing (see Figure 11-7). The salt is a random piece of data that adds entropy to the password making them much harder to brute force or perform a dictionary attack. Salting a password makes their cracking much harder to perform, but as we just stated, with GPU hardware increasing in power each year, what is a safe password today, could be cracked and compromised in a few short years.

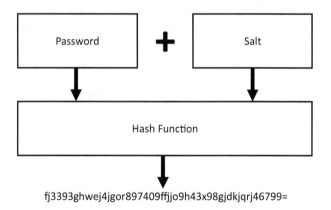

fj3393ghwej4jgor897409ffjjo9h43x98gjdkjqrj46799=

Figure 11-7. *Adding a salt to a password before hashing*

The next option is to use a variation of the salted hash using a technique called a password-based key derivation function, or PBKDF2 for short (see Figure 11-8). This is conceptually the same as what we just discussed with a salt added with the password, but the main difference is you specify a "number of iterations" parameter. This parameter is the number of times the hash is repeated. So, if that number was 10, then the password and salt combination is hashed ten times. The intention with this iteration parameter is to slow down the hashing process, which means if someone gets a copy of your password table, instead of performing billions of passwords hash cracks per second you drastically reduce the number that can be attempted per second making the cracking process much less desirable to a would-be hacker.

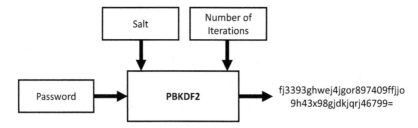

Figure 11-8. *Password-based key derivation functions*

Using a password-based key derivation function puts us in a good position, but where does Key Vault fit into this? Adding a Key Vault into the equation gives us a bit of extra protection. When using a PBKDF2 function, we have to provide a salt and a "number of iterations" parameter; both need to be presented when hashing a password to compare against a stored password. Conventionally, the salt, of which you would use a new salt per password, would be stored in a database and the number of iterations might be a configuration option. The salt is not a key that is used for confidentiality. But why make it easy for an attacker? Using Key Vault, we can encrypt the salt before we store it in the database (see Figure 11-9). Then when a user authenticates onto your system, the salt first needs to be decrypted using Key Vault before the password hash is recalculated.

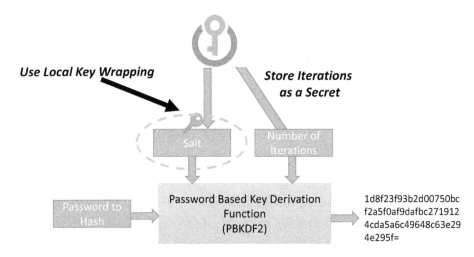

Figure 11-9. *Using Key Vault to protect salts and iteration values*

To successfully create a hash for a password to match a hash in your passwords table, you also need to specify the same number of iterations. If your stored password was hashed with 1000 iterations and a salt, and you try to hash the same password with the same salt, but 1001 iterations, the hash will not match. This means the number of iterations is a configuration item, which is a perfect candidate to store as a secret in Key Vault. As with the salt, hiding the number of iterations isn't part of the security of a PBKDF, but why make it easy for an attacker, by storing the number of iterations as an encrypted secret in the vault, you are making their lives just that bit harder if they get hold of your hashed password tables as they not only have to decrypt the salt, but they have also to figure out the correct number of iterations to use, which is safely stored in the vault.

Let's look at using the password-based key derivation function with the Azure Key Vault.

In Chapter 5, I introduced the code required to perform a password-based key derivation function to hash a password. This code remains the same, as seen in the following.

```
public class PBKDF2
{
    public static byte[] HashPassword(byte[] toBeHashed, byte[] salt,
                        int numberOfRounds)
```

```
    {
        using (var rfc2898 = new Rfc2898DeriveBytes(
                        toBeHashed, salt, numberOfRounds))
        {
            return rfc2898.GetBytes(20);
        }
    }
}
```

The password hashing method takes a byte array of the data that we want to hash followed by a byte array containing the salt value, then finally we have an integer representing the number of iterations to be used for the hashing function. The hashing itself is done using the Rfc2898DeriveBytes class where you provide all three of the parameters passed into our helper method. Then to calculate the hash we call GetBytes(20) on the Rfc2898DeriveBytes instance. The reason we generate 20 bytes is because the Rfc2898DeriveBytes class uses SHA-1 internally, which gives a 120-bit hash code, or 20 bytes. This helper method still forms the basis for our password hashing, so let's now see what that looks like when we use Key Vault to encrypt the salt and store the number of iterations as a secret.

The following code uses our PBKDF2 helper class and the Azure Key Vault sample framework we introduced in Chapter 10.

```
class Program
{
    public static async Task Main(string[] args)
    {
        await KeyVault();
    }

    public static async Task KeyVault()
    {
        IKeyVault vault = new KeyVault();

        const string MY_KEY_NAME = "StephenHauntsKey";
        const string ITERATIONS_VALUE = "PBKDF2Iterations";

        string keyId = await vault.CreateKeyAsync(MY_KEY_NAME);
```

```csharp
// Encrypt our salt with Key Vault and Store it in the       database
byte[] salt = SecureRandom.GenerateRandomNumber(32);

byte[] encryptedSalt = await vault.EncryptAsync(keyId, salt);

var iterationsId = await vault.SetSecretAsync(
                ITERATIONS_VALUE, "20000");

// Get our encrypted salt from the database and
// decrypt it with the Key Vault.
byte[] decryptedSalt = await vault.DecryptAsync(keyId, encryptedSalt);

int iterations = int.Parse(
        await vault.GetSecretAsync(ITERATIONS_VALUE));

// Hash our password with a PBKDF2
string password = "Pa55w0rd";

byte[] hashedPassword = PBKDF2.HashPassword(
    Encoding.ASCII.GetBytes(password),
    decryptedSalt, iterations);

Console.WriteLine("Hashed Password : " +
                Convert.ToBase64String(hashedPassword));

// Remove HSM backed key
await vault.DeleteKeyAsync(MY_KEY_NAME);
Console.WriteLine("Key Deleted : " + keyId);
    }
}
```

Let's break this down piece by piece. First, we want to instantiate our Key Vault class and create a key to use for this example.

```csharp
IKeyVault vault = new KeyVault();

const string MY_KEY_NAME = "MyKey";
const string ITERATIONS_VALUE = "PBKDF2Iterations";

string keyId = await vault.CreateKeyAsync(MY_KEY_NAME);
```

There are also a couple of constant strings that define the key name to use in the vault and the name of the secret where we store the number of iterations to use.

```
byte[] salt = SecureRandom.GenerateRandomNumber(32);

byte[] encryptedSalt = await vault.EncryptAsync(keyId, salt);
var iterationsId = await vault.SetSecretAsync(ITERATIONS_VALUE, "20000");
```

The next task is to generate a 32-byte salt using the random number generator we have used throughout the book and store it in a byte array. The salt is encrypted with Key Vault using the key we just created. The result of this encryption operation is stored in a byte array where it could be converted to a base64 string and stored in a database for use later. Next, we store the number of iterations to use as a secret in Key Vault. For this example, we set this to 20,000. We now have everything we need in place to perform our secure password hashing.

If we want to hash a password, we have to perform a few steps before we do the hash. First, we need to decrypt the salt and then retrieve the number of iterations parameter from the Vault. These steps are done with the following lines of code.

```
byte[] decryptedSalt = await vault.DecryptAsync(keyId, encryptedSalt);

int iterations = int.Parse(await vault.GetSecretAsync(ITERATIONS_VALUE));
```

Now we have everything we need to perform the password hash, which is what the following lines of code do.

```
string password = "Pa55w0rd";

byte[] hashedPassword = PBKDF2.HashPassword(
                Encoding.UTF8.GetBytes(password),
                decryptedSalt, iterations);
```

The password we want to hash is stored in a string, which we first need to convert to a byte array by using `Encoding.UTF8.GetBytes()`. We then pass in the decrypted salt value and the number of iterations from Key Vault. When this is finished running, we get our hashed password returned as a byte array where we can convert it to a base64 string and store it in our database next to our encrypted salt.

Let's now imagine the scenario that the hashed password and salt has been stolen from our database and is in the hands of our attacker. What can they do? Well, first they do not have access to the original salt value, only the encrypted salt value. To decrypt the salt, they need direct access to your system, network, and Azure subscription to decrypt the salt value. Not only do they need to decrypt the salt value, but they also have no idea what iteration value you used, to try and guess would take a vast amount of time per password so not be worth it for the attacker. Again, to get access to this iteration value, they need access to your Key Vault and Azure subscription. Protecting the salt and the iteration value is not a requirement for PBKDF2; its security benefit comes from slowing down the hashing process. But why make it easy for an attacker if you have a Key Vault available? It adds an extra layer of security to your password process.

Varying the Iterations over Time

Selecting a value for the number of iterations parameter is an application design decision where you need to trade off overall security with the usability of your application. The higher the number of iterations the more secure your passwords is against attack, but the slower your application will be when calculating the hash. Another aspect you need to consider is increasing the number of iterations over time. Let's assume that you use an iteration count of 5,000 currently for your passwords. Over the course of a few years, GPU performance increases exponentially, and you decide that you want to increase that counter.

For new passwords, this is easy, as people sign up to your service you use the new iteration count, but for existing passwords in your database, they have to be checked using their existing iterations count until you rehash that password. Using Key Vault makes this easy because as you add a secret for an iteration count, you can store the secret ID from the vault against a password along with the encrypted salt. This means that your password table looks something like Table 11-1.

Table 11-1. *Example Mappings of Key to Salt and Iteration Secret*

Hashed Password	Encrypted Salt	Key ID	Iteration Secret ID
vwryjr9w8e8rj7w9c=	xeirnwyrn98wn59834579=	uri to key	Secret ID 1
mboewwoirutmoru=	92dgh5498509erwt80n9n9=	uri to key	Secret ID 1
94jgje9er9e8gmcew=	6rotumew9rcuwjn8665g9k=	uri to key	Secret ID 1
hew93w0euf4gjrj4t=	29rgve9erwvker9t8493884=	uri to key	Secret ID 2

The first column is where we store the result of the PBKDF2 hash. If the table is stolen, this is the hash that the attack will try to reverse. The next column contains the encrypted salt. Before the password hash can be recalculated and checked, this salt first needs to be decrypted using the key stored at the URL in the Key ID column. As we already discussed, this adds an extra challenge to the attacker as they need to decrypt that salt before they can use it. In the final column, we have the URL to the secret that stores the iteration count. The first three rows in the table all have an ID to a secret that contains the same iteration count. Let's assume that is 5000. At a point in time, the decision was made to raise this iteration count to 20,000, and this is illustrated in the final row where the ID for the iteration count secret is now pointing at a new secret. For every new password that is entered into the system, you can store it with the new iteration secret URL.

Using a technique like that is fine for new accounts created in the system. But what do you do if you want to bring everyone else along? That depends on how quickly you want to update everyone, which is an application design decision.

One way to approach this is the next time someone with an older iteration count password logs in, you could take them down a password reset route, so you deliberately force them to enter a new password and then overwrite the record in the database once you have authenticated their existing password. Also, instead of making them type in a new password you could rehash their existing password that they have typed in once you have authenticated their existing password. Using this would be transparent to them behind the scenes, but it is a way to gradually bring your users passwords up to date with the new passwords hashing iteration count as mandated by your organization. How you go about bringing people in line with the new password policy is to be decided between your system and security architects.

The main software development principle we are introducing here is that you are storing a secret ID for each password, which gives you the ability to vary the iteration count and encryption keys for the salt as needed, which provides a lot of flexibility over time to change your password hashing policies.

Digital Signing

The final pattern to look at with the Azure Key Vault is creating and verifying digital signatures. We looked at digital signatures in Chapter 8, where we performed the signing and verification tasks using the `RSAPKCS1SignatureFormatter` and

RSAPKCS1SignatoreDeFormatter classes in the .NET Framework. Signing and verification of data is a feature that Key Vault offers as part of its standard functionality, and it is straightforward to do, which reduces the complexity in doing it yourself using the RSAPKCS1SignatureFormatter and DeFormatter classes. Let's look at this as an example.

```
public class Hash
{
    public static byte[] Sha256(byte[] toBeHashed)
    {
        using (var sha256 = SHA256.Create())
        {
            return sha256.ComputeHash(toBeHashed);
        }
    }
}
```

The first helper method that we reuse from Chapter 4 is the SHA-256 hashing function. We create the digital signatures on a hash of our data as opposed to the data itself. To create a digital signature with Key Vault is very easy, as illustrated in the following code.

```
class Program
{
    public static async Task Main(string[] args)
    {
        await KeyVault();
    }

    public static async Task KeyVault()
    {
        IKeyVault vault = new KeyVault();

        const string MY_KEY_NAME = "StephenHauntsKey";
        string keyId = await vault.CreateKeyAsync(MY_KEY_NAME);

        string importantDocument = "Important data to sign.";
```

```
    byte[] documentDigest = Hash.Sha256(
            Encoding.UTF8.GetBytes(importantDocument));

    byte[] signature = await vault.Sign(keyId, documentDigest);

    bool verified = await vault.Verify(keyId, documentDigest,
    signature);

    // Remove HSM backed key
    await vault.DeleteKeyAsync(MY_KEY_NAME);
    Console.WriteLine("Key Deleted : " + keyId);
  }
}
```

Let's go through the code bit by bit. First, we want to create our instance of Key Vault helper class and create a key.

```
IKeyVault vault = new KeyVault();

const string MY_KEY_NAME = "StephenHauntsKey";
string keyId = await vault.CreateKeyAsync(MY_KEY_NAME);
```

Once we have created the key for the example code, we can define the data we want to create a digital signature for. In this case, it is just a simple string, but it could easily be a file or any block of memory. Before we create the digital signature, we want to create a hash of the data. We first convert the string into a byte array using the `Encoding.UTF8.GetBytes()` helper method from .NET. We then pass the byte array of our data into the `Sha256()` method on our `Hash` helper class. This returns a byte array containing the SHA-256 hash.

```
string importantDocument = "Important data to sign.";

byte[] documentDigest = Hash.Sha256(
      Encoding.UTF8.GetBytes(importantDocument));
```

Next, we want to create our digital signature, which is very easy to do with Key Vault.

```
byte[] signature = await vault.Sign(keyId, documentDigest);
```

We do this simply by calling the `Sign` method on our vault helper class and provide the keyId that we just created and the hash of our data. This calls out to Key Vault, generates the digital signature, and returns it as a byte array. If you want to verify that the signature is valid to prove that the original data hasn't been tampered with, then you call the `Verify` method on Key Vault helper class.

```
bool verified = await vault.Verify(keyId, documentDigest, signature);
```

If the data hasn't been tampered with, and it is a valid digital signature, `true` is returned; otherwise, `false` is returned. Now that we have looked at how to perform a digital signature signing and verification with the Azure Key Vault, let's take our original hybrid encryption example from Chapter 9 and upgrade it to use Key Vault.

Upgrading the Hybrid Encryption Example

At the end of Chapter 9, we had built a fairly extensive sample project that combined many of the cryptographic primitives to create a hybrid encryption scheme (see Figure 11-10).

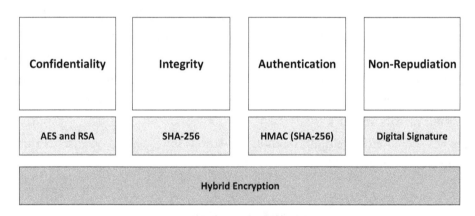

Figure 11-10. *Cryptography primitives used for hybrid encryption*

This meant we used the AES and RSA algorithms for confidentiality, SHA-256 to provide integrity, HMAC (SHA-256) to provide authentication, and digital signatures to provide non-repudiation. Before we look at upgrading the example from Chapter 9 to use Azure Key Vault, let's remind ourselves how the hybrid encryption scheme works by using our two actors: Alice and Bob (see Figure 11-11).

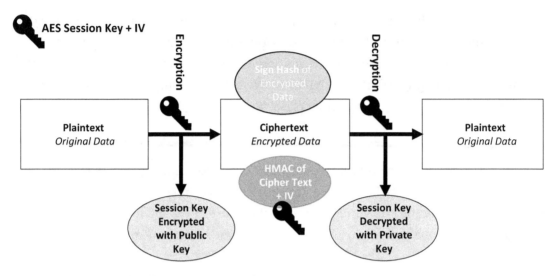

Figure 11-11. *Hybrid encryption with HMACS and digital signatures*

First, **Alice** is going to send a message to **Bob** using hybrid encryption with built-in integrity checking and a digital signature.

Alice generates a new 256-bit (32-byte) AES session key.

Alice then generates a new 128-bit (16-byte) initialization vector.

Alice then encrypts her message with AES using the session key and the IV.

Alice encrypts the session key with RSA and **Bob's** public key.

Alice calculates the HMAC of the encrypted data and initialization vector combined using the unencrypted AES session key as the key for the HMAC, which means that the recipient can only recalculate the same hash once they have decrypted the AES session key with their private key.

Alice now calculates the digital signature of the HMAC, which we just created, using her private signing key (see Figure 11-12).

> **Encrypted Data Packet**
>
> RSA Encrypted Session Key
> AES Initialization Vector
> AES Encrypted Data
> HMAC (SHA-256) of Encrypted Data
> Digital Signature of HMAC

Figure 11-12. *Packet of information used for the hybrid encryption*

196

Alice stores the encrypted data, encrypted AES session key, initialization vector, and digital signature in a separate structure or file. This is the packet of data that is sent to **Bob**.

Once **Bob** has this packet of information, he wants to decrypt it.

To do this, he uses the following process.

Bob decrypts the encrypted AES session key by using RSA and his private key.

Bob recalculates the HMAC of the encrypted data and initialization vector using the decrypted AES session key.

Bob compares his HMAC to the HMAC sent with the message. If the HMAC fields match, then the data is intact, and it is safe to decrypt the message.

The reverse operation is true if Bob wants to send a reply back to Alice. If we look at this process, there are two areas that we can replace with operations to Key Vault. The first is the initial RSA encryption of the local AES session key. This is the same principle as the local key wrapping pattern. The second area that we can switch to Key Vault is the generation and verification of the digital signatures.

From the existing example, we reuse the `AesEncryption` helper methods. It is not worth going through them again, but we also reuse the `EncryptedPacket` class.

```
public class EncryptedPacket
{
    public byte[] EncryptedSessionKey;
    public byte[] EncryptedData;
    public byte[] Iv;
    public byte[] Hmac;
    public byte[] Signature;
}
```

In this class, we store the results of the hybrid encryption. The first member is `EncryptedSessionKey`, which is the local AES key encrypted by Key Vault. The next member is the `EncryptedData`, which contains the data that is encrypted with AES, just like in the example from Chapter 9. Then we have the IV field, which is the initialization vector that we generate for using with AES; this is also the same as the example in Chapter 9. Then we have the `Hmac` field, which is the HMAC of our encrypted data and the initialization vector combined. We include the initialization vector in this hash because we want to know if someone has tampered with the IV. Finally, we have the Signature field, which is the digital signature created from our HMAC. This is the second part, which we will switch out to use Key Vault.

Let's now modify the HybridEncrytion class from Chapter 9 to use Key Vault. First, we store a reference to the KeyVault instance that is passed into the constructor, and we create an instance of the AesEncryption class.

```
public class HybridEncryption
{
    readonly IKeyVault _keyVault;
    readonly AesEncryption _aes = new AesEncryption();

    public HybridEncryption(IKeyVault keyVault)
    {
        _keyVault = keyVault;
    }
}
```

Now we want to modify the original EncryptData method to upgrade it to use Key Vault; which is demonstrated in the following code.

```
public EncryptedPacket EncryptData(byte[] original, string keyId)
{
    var sessionKey = _aes.GenerateRandomNumber(32);

    var encryptedPacket = new EncryptedPacket
    {
        Iv = _aes.GenerateRandomNumber(16)
    };

    encryptedPacket.EncryptedData = _aes.Encrypt(original, sessionKey,
            encryptedPacket.Iv);

    encryptedPacket.EncryptedSessionKey =
            _keyVault.EncryptAsync(keyId, sessionKey).Result;

    using (var hmac = new HMACSHA256(sessionKey))
    {
        encryptedPacket.Hmac = hmac.ComputeHash(
                Combine(encryptedPacket.EncryptedData,
                encryptedPacket.Iv));
    }
```

```
encryptedPacket.Signature =
        _keyVault.Sign(keyId, encryptedPacket.Hmac).Result;

return encryptedPacket;
}
```

Let's break the encryption process down into smaller steps. First, we want to generate our local AES session key and initialization vector. This doesn't change from the original example in Chapter 9.

```
var sessionKey = _aes.GenerateRandomNumber(32);

var encryptedPacket = new EncryptedPacket
{
        Iv = _aes.GenerateRandomNumber(16)
};
```

Now we have the AES session key and initialization vector we can go ahead and encrypt our data using the AES helper method. The encryption is happening all locally with no jumps to Key Vault yet. The encrypted data is then placed into our encrypted packet ready to be sent to the recipient.

```
encryptedPacket.EncryptedData = _aes.Encrypt(
                original, sessionKey, encryptedPacket.Iv);
```

Once we have encrypted our data, we can go ahead and encrypt the AES key using Key Vault, which is the first change from performing the RSA encryption ourselves. In this example, we are using a key ID that is passed into the EncryptData method. Once we have encrypted that session key, it is placed into the encrypted packet data structure.

```
encryptedPacket.EncryptedSessionKey =
                _keyVault.EncryptAsync(keyId, sessionKey).Result;
```

Our next step in the process is to calculate the HMAC based on the SHA-256 hashing algorithm. For the HMAC we need to provide a key, and in this case, we provide the unencrypted AES key. By doing this, it means the recipient needs to decrypt the key with Key Vault before they can recalculate the hash.

```
using (var hmac = new HMACSHA256(sessionKey))
{
    encryptedPacket.Hmac = hmac.ComputeHash(
                Combine(encryptedPacket.EncryptedData,
                encryptedPacket.Iv));
}
```

When we create the HMAC, we first combine the encrypted data along with the initialization vector. This means we can detect if the original data and the initialization vector were tampered with. The HMAC hash is also stored in the encrypted packet, which is sent to the recipient of the data. The final step in the process is to create a digital signature of the data now; this is the second part that is different to the original example in Chapter 9.

```
encryptedPacket.Signature =
            _keyVault.Sign(keyId, encryptedPacket.Hmac).Result;
```

The digital signature is created by calling the Sign method and providing the keyId to use for Key Vault and the hash of the data we want to sign. The resulting digital signature is placed into the encrypted packet data structure. That concludes the EncryptData method for encrypting, hashing, and signing the data. Let's now look at the DecryptData method, which decrypts the data and check everything is valid. The complete method is shown next.

```
public byte[] DecryptData(
            EncryptedPacket encryptedPacket, string keyId)
{
    var decryptedSessionKey = _keyVault.DecryptAsync( keyId,
            encryptedPacket.EncryptedSessionKey).Result;

    using (var hmac = new HMACSHA256(decryptedSessionKey))
    {
        var hmacToCheck = hmac.ComputeHash(
                    Combine(encryptedPacket.EncryptedData,
                        encryptedPacket.Iv));

        if (!Compare(encryptedPacket.Hmac, hmacToCheck))
        {
```

```
                throw new CryptographicException(
                    "HMAC for does not match encrypted packet.");
            }

            if (!_keyVault.Verify(keyId,
                            encryptedPacket.Hmac,
                            encryptedPacket.Signature).Result)
            {
                throw new CryptographicException(
                    "Digital Signature can not be verified.");
            }
        }

        var decryptedData = _aes.Decrypt(
                        encryptedPacket.EncryptedData,
                        decryptedSessionKey,
                        encryptedPacket.Iv);

    return decryptedData;
}
```

Let's again break this method down bit by bit. First, we need to recover the AES session key that we need to decrypt our data and recalculate our HMAC. This is done by calling the DecryptAsync method on Key Vault helper class, and it needs the keyId to be supplied along with the encrypted session key.

```
var decryptedSessionKey = _keyVault.DecryptAsync(
        keyId, encryptedPacket.EncryptedSessionKey).Result;
```

Once this call has completed, we have the recovered AES key, so we can then check the HMAC and decrypt our data. First, we recalculate the HMAC by using the decrypted key. Again, the HMAC is calculated on the combination of the AES encrypted data and the initialization vector. We then compare the newly created HMAC to the one we had stored in the encrypted packet. If they match, we carry on, but if they don't, we throw a CryptographicException and bail out.

```
using (var hmac = new HMACSHA256(decryptedSessionKey))
{
    var hmacToCheck = hmac.ComputeHash(
```

```
                Combine(encryptedPacket.EncryptedData,
                      encryptedPacket.Iv));

    if (!Compare(encryptedPacket.Hmac, hmacToCheck))
    {
        throw new CryptographicException(
            "HMAC for does not match encrypted packet.");
    }

    if (!_keyVault.Verify(keyId,
                    encryptedPacket.Hmac,
                    encryptedPacket.Signature).Result)
    {
        throw new CryptographicException(
                "Digital Signature can not be verified.");
    }
}
```

Once we are happy with the HMAC, we then make another call into Key Vault with the `Verify` method, to check the validity of our digital signature. The signature is being checked against the HMAC and signature fields provided in our encrypted packet object. If the `Verify` method returns true, then we are good to carry on and decrypt our data. If the `Verify` method returns false, then we again throw a `CryptographicException` and bail out.

```
var decryptedData = _aes.Decrypt(encryptedPacket.EncryptedData,
                    decryptedSessionKey,
                    encryptedPacket.Iv);
```

Once all of these checks have been passed, we are confident that the data hasn't been corrupted or tampered with, so we can go ahead and decrypt our original data with the recovered AES Key. This is a local AES operation, so Key Vault isn't called.

Now that we have upgraded the `HybridEncryption` class, we need to call it. The following is the complete code.

```
class Program
{
    public static async Task Main(string[] args)
    {
        await KeyVault();
    }

    public static async Task KeyVault()
    {
        const string original = "Very secret information.";

        IKeyVault vault = new KeyVault();

        const string MY_KEY_NAME = "MyKey";
        string keyId =
                await vault.CreateKeyAsync(MY_KEY_NAME);

        var hybrid = new HybridEncryption(vault);

        Console.WriteLine("Hybrid Encryption with Key Vault");
        Console.WriteLine("--------------------------------");
        Console.WriteLine();

        try
        {
            var encryptedBlock = hybrid.EncryptData(
                    Encoding.UTF8.GetBytes(original), keyId);

            var decrpyted = hybrid.DecryptData(
                            encryptedBlock, keyId);

            Console.WriteLine("Original Message = " + original);

            Console.WriteLine();
            Console.WriteLine("Message After Decryption = "
                    + Encoding.UTF8.GetString(decrpyted));
        }
```

```
        catch (CryptographicException ex)
        {
            Console.WriteLine("Error : " + ex.Message);
        }

        Console.ReadLine();
    }
}
```

Let's break it down into the most relevant sections. First, we have a string that contains the data we want to encrypt and send to our recipient. In this example, it's a string, but it could just as easily be a file or any other data. The next step is to create an instance of our KeyVault helper class and create a key, which we have called MyKey.

```
const string original = "Very secret information.";

IKeyVault vault = new KeyVault();

const string MY_KEY_NAME = "MyKey";
string keyId = await vault.CreateKeyAsync(MY_KEY_NAME);

var hybrid = new HybridEncryption(vault);
```

Once we have created the key, we create an instance of HybridEncryption and pass in our KeyVault instance; which means that our HybridEncryption class knows which connection to Key Vault to use.

Now that we have created a key and set up the HybridEncryption class, we now want to encrypt some data.

```
var encryptedBlock = hybrid.EncryptData(
                Encoding.UTF8.GetBytes(original), keyId);

var decrpyted = hybrid.DecryptData(encryptedBlock, keyId);
```

The encryption and decryption process is now nice and easy. First, we convert the data that we want to encrypt, which in this case is a string, to a byte array and pass it into the EncryptData method along with the key ID for Key Vault key we have just created. Once this method has finished executing, our encrypted package instance is returned to be sent to a recipient.

In this case, we are going to decrypt it right away by calling `DecryptData` and passing the encrypted packet and the key again, which gives the original data back. The example code then displays the original data and the decrypted data to the terminal window, so we can see that is has worked as illustrated in Figure 11-13.

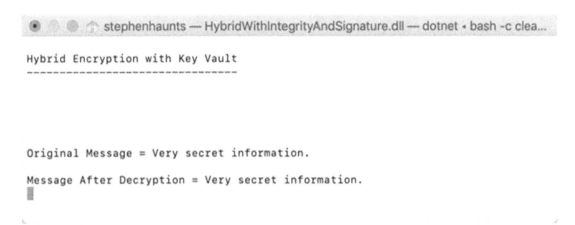

Figure 11-13. *Results of running the updated hybrid encryption example*

That concludes our look at the Azure Key vault and the upgrade to our hybrid encryption example from Chapter 9.

Summary

In this chapter, we looked at a series of usage patterns for using the Azure Key Vault that included multiple environments, configuration as secrets, local key wrapping, password protection, and digital signing. These simple but powerful patterns allow you to get the most out of using Key Vault. On the face of it, Key Vault is a simple service to use, but with a few simple operations, as you have seen, it opens up a lot of possibilities to use encryption in your software solutions with robust and secure key management.

Using the ideas around local key wrapping, you can also drastically reduce the costs of using Key Vault, because in a session you can request to decrypt a local symmetric key, which you use in-memory to encrypt and decrypt data. That means you can reduce the number of hops you have to do to Key Vault and therefore reducing the cost.

In the final chapter of this book, we recap what we learned and look toward the future of security.

CHAPTER 12

Final Summary

The central reason that I wrote this book was to educate developers on why data breaches are inevitable. Although organizations protect their data centers and databases to the best of their abilities, the grim reality is that data breaches still happen, whether they are outside jobs or initiated from the inside by staff. In this final chapter.

Accepting the inevitability of data breaches is a fundamental mindset change that developers and companies need to make with data breaches. We need to focus our efforts on making sure that if a data breach does occur, it is a secure breach. With this, I mean that the essential data within the data breach such as personally identifiable information (PII), financial information, or anything that can be used for an attack for their gain is encrypted and the encryption keys are securely protected.

This book is aimed squarely at developers who build software for their organizations. The purpose of the book isn't to try and turn you into a master cryptographer, but to allow you to make use of the tools that are available to you in the .NET Framework/.NET Core to add additional security to your systems.

As I was planning this book, I could have taken a few directions. I could have written a long and extensive reference manual where I document every property or method on all the relevant classes in .NET, but that would have been a very long book, which replicates a lot of the documentation that is already available on the Internet. I don't like books like that and instead wanted to develop a practical book that takes you through the cryptographic principles available and builds up a working sample application as the book evolves. I have purposefully tried to make this book as short, yet information dense as possible. As a software developer who has worked for many large enterprises, I fully understand that projects and products are developed under time and budget constraints, and it can be quite common that some security measures in our applications can be deprioritized over more physical and more visible features. By reading this book, I hope I have given you the tools to be able to incorporate more encryption and security into your applications quickly to try and avoid having complex security deprioritized.

Let's go through a summary of what we have learned in this book.

© Stephen Haunts 2019
S. Haunts, *Applied Cryptography in .NET and Azure Key Vault*,
https://doi.org/10.1007/978-1-4842-4375-6_12

Cryptography Summary

Throughout history, cryptography has played a crucial part in helping people, companies, and governments keep secrets. In the early days of cryptography, the encryption process worked on simple text based messages, but as the digital revolution took hold, encryption has been against binary data. In the modern world, you cannot get through the day without cryptography playing some part in your life from securing your Wi-Fi network, protecting data on your mobile devices or buying a product from online retailers. With great innovation comes threats and one of our most significant risks is data being stolen from organizations and used against people to impersonate them and potentially con them out of money. We explored the four main pillars of modern cryptography: confidentiality, integrity, authentication, and non-repudiation.

Confidentiality is what you associate with cryptography and encryption, where you take data and encrypt it so it is in a form that cannot be read by someone else.

Data integrity is about maintaining and proving the accuracy and the consistency of data sent between two parties. This means that if someone sends data to a third party, the individual should be able to detect if the data has been corrupted or tampered with.

Authentication is establishing the identity of a person or system sending a message. A good example is with TLS certificates on a web server proving the identity of the server that you wish to connect to. Use of a cryptographic key authenticates the identity. Having a less secure key means there is lower trust between two parties. Authentication is also commonly used by everyone when they enter their username and password to gain access to a system. Your Facebook or Twitter account is an excellent example of this. To use those systems, you have to authenticate yourself with the Facebook or the Twitter website to prove who you are.

Non-repudiation is proving that someone has carried out an action or signed a document. A signature on a paper contract is an excellent example of this. If a contract has been signed and witnessed, then that person cannot deny having signed the agreement.

Random Numbers

When we started our look at cryptography in .NET, we began by looking at random numbers. Secure random numbers are essential to modern cryptography as we depend on this ability to create encryption lets for our symmetric algorithms like AES, keys for HMAC and salts for password hashing. The most common random number generator in .NET is the `System.Random` class, but while this is fine for generating a set of lottery numbers or simulating a dice roll, the results it produces are very deterministic unless you provide a different seed value every time. The ideal random number generator to use in the .NET ecosystem is the `RngCryptoServiceProvider` that offers a cryptographically secure means of generating non-deterministic random numbers for encryption keys.

Hashing and Authentication

The next primitives were hashing and authenticated hashing. Hashing is a one-way algorithm that generates a unique fingerprint (hash code) of a piece of input data. Once a hash code has been generated for a piece of data, it should be infeasible to reverse the hash to get back to the original value. To be considered a reliable and useful hash function, it must conform to three main properties:

- The hash code must be easy to calculate for any input message.

- You should not be able to create a message that has a specified hash code.

- Any changes to the original message should completely change the hash code.

You should not be able to find two input messages that result in the same hash code. Another way to frame the concept of a hash function is to think of it as the digital equivalent of a fingerprint for a piece of data. Once you have generated a hash code for that piece of data, the hash code is always the same if you calculate it again, unless the original data changes in any way, no matter how small that difference is.

The process of calculating a hash code (or message digest) of an item of data is straightforward to do in the .NET Framework or .NET Core. There are different algorithms you can use in .NET such as MD5, SHA-1, SHA-256, and SHA-512. The properties of hashing, such as only being able to hash in one direction and the hash code is unique to a piece of data, makes hashing the perfect mechanism for checking the integrity of data. The integrity checking means when you send data across a network to someone else, you can use hashing as a way to tell if the original data has been tampered with or corrupted.

Before sending the data, you calculate a hash of the data to get its unique fingerprint. You then send that data and the hash to the recipient. They then compute the hash of the data they have received, and then compare it to the hash you sent. If the generated hash codes are identical, then the data has been successfully received without data loss or corruption. If the hash codes fail to match up correctly, then the data received is not the same as the data initially sent.

For the examples in this book, we used the secure hash based on generating a 256-bit (32-byte) hash code (SHA-256). If you need to use a higher strength hash, you can swap out the hashing code to use SHA-512 because the coding interfaces are the same between them.

Authenticated Hashing

For hashing, we settled on the SHA (Secure Hash Algorithm) family of hashing functions. The purpose is to provide integrity checking capabilities within our applications to help us detect if data has been tampered with or corrupted over time. We then looked at satisfying another of our four pillars of cryptography by talking about authentication, which is a natural follow on from integrity.

If you combine a one-way hash function with a secret cryptographic key, you get a hash message authentication code (HMAC). Like a hash code, an HMAC is used to verify the integrity of a message. A HMAC also allows you to verify the authentication of that message because only a person who knows the key can calculate the same hash of the message. The fundamental differences between a standard MD5 or SHA hash and a HMAC, anyone can calculate a hash code using MD5 or SHA and get the same results for a piece of data. Only an authorized individual can generate the same hash code using an HMAC because they need to have the same key that was used to create the original HMAC hash code.

Storing Passwords

Storing passwords in a database is a very common task for our systems to perform, but this task is so commonly done badly that it leaves the integrity of our systems exposed when passwords are leaked in a data breach. We started our exploration of securely storing passwords by examining some of the bad ways to do it. Let's remind ourselves of these bad techniques.

The first and the worst solution is to store passwords as plaintext in a database. Doing this offers no protection at all should your database tables get leaked in a data breach. Sadly, there are a lot of old websites out there that do use this plaintext technique, but for a new system under your control, you should never do this.

The next technique that we looked at, which is better than plaintext passwords is basic hashing of passwords. A hash is a one-way function, where once a password has been hashed, you shouldn't be able to go back the other way to recover the password. This principle works in theory, but plain hashed passwords are relatively easy to recover by performing either a brute-force attack or a rainbow table/dictionary attack. Many people use simple passwords, such as a spouse's name or a pet's name, which are very susceptible to attack. If you use a long and complex passphrase, you are afforded a little more protection, but not by much. Modern password cracking tools like Hashcat are designed to use the powerful graphics processing units (GPUs) built into modern graphics cards. These GPU cards allow tools like Hashcat to perform billions of hashing operations per second and as these graphics cards get more powerful each year, standard hashed passwords get easier to crack.

To try and remedy the ease of cracking hashed passwords the next technique builds on hashing by the inclusion of a salt to the password before hashing. The salt is a random piece of data that adds entropy to the password making them much harder to brute force or perform a dictionary attack. Salting a password makes their cracking much harder to perform, but with GPU hardware power increasing every year, what is considered a safe password today, could be cracked and compromised in a few short years.

The final option was a variation of the salted hash using a technique called a Password Based Key Derivation Function (PBKDF2). The main difference, compared to a SHA hash, is you specify a "number of iterations" parameter. This parameter is the number of times the hash is repeated. So, if that number was 10, then the password and salt combination is hashed ten times. The intention with this iteration parameter is to slow down the hashing process which means if someone does get a copy of your password table, instead of performing billions of passwords hash cracks per second you drastically reduce the number that can be attempted per second making the cracking process much less desirable to a would-be hacker. The .NET object that we used to generate one of these PBKDF2 password hashes was `Rfc2898DeriveBytes`.

Symmetric Encryption

We have discussed how hashing and hashed message authentication codes are one-way operations. Once you hash some data, you shouldn't be able to reverse the hash to go back to the original data. Symmetric encryption algorithms, on the other hand, are a two-way operation where you use the same key for both encryption and decryption of your message; you can reverse the encryption process to recover the original data provided you use the same key, which is why it is referred to as *symmetric*.

Symmetric encryption has both advantages and disadvantages to its use.

Advantage: Very Secure

When using a secure algorithm, symmetric encryption is exceptionally secure. One of the most widely-used symmetric key encryption systems is the Advanced Encryption Standard (AES). As of the writing of this book, AES is unbroken, so it is one of the recommended algorithms.

Advantage: Fast

One of the problems with public key encryption systems like RSA is that they need complicated mathematics to work, making them very computationally intensive and slow. Encrypting and decrypting symmetric key data is easier, which provides excellent read and write performance. Many solid-state drives, which are very fast, use symmetric key encryption store data, yet they are still a lot faster than unencrypted standard hard drives.

Disadvantage: Sharing Keys Is Hard

One of the most significant problems with symmetric key encryption algorithms is that you need to have a way to get the key to the person with who you are sending the encrypted data. Encryption keys aren't simple strings of text like passwords; they are byte arrays of randomly generated data, such as the random numbers we generated with RNGCryptoServiceProvider earlier in this book. As such, you need to have a safe way to get the key to the other person.

With this in mind, symmetric key encryption is particularly useful when encrypting your information as opposed to when sharing encrypted information. There are ways to use the power of symmetric encryption with a suitable key sharing scheme, which we looked at earlier in the book when we talk about hybrid encryption schemes.

Disadvantage: Dangerous If Compromised

When someone gets hold of one of your symmetric keys, they can decrypt everything encrypted with that key. When you're using symmetric encryption for two-way communications, this means that both sides of the conversation get compromised. With asymmetrical public-key cryptography like RSA, someone that gets your private key can decrypt messages sent to you but can't decrypt what you send to the other party since it is encrypted with a different key pair.

In this book, we explored three types of symmetric encryption algorithm, DES, Triple DES, and AES. DES and Triple DES should be treated as legacy algorithms, but it was still worth discussing them because there are a lot of old systems out there that still encrypt their data with DES or Triple DES. If you are working on a newer system that doesn't have these legacy constraints, then you should use AES by default.

AES offers three key sizes: 128 bits (16 bytes), 192 bits (24 bytes), and 256 bits (32 bytes). The examples in this book used the 256-bit key size, and we used the `AesCryptoServiceProvider` class to perform our AES encryption.

Asymmetric Encryption

Symmetric encryption is a two-way encryption process that uses the same key for both encryption and decryption of your message. The main problem with symmetric encryption is that of securely sharing keys. For a recipient to decrypt a message, they need the same key as the sender, and this exchange of keys can be difficult to do securely. An excellent solution to this problem is to use asymmetric cryptography, which is also referred to as public key cryptography.

With public key cryptography, you have two keys; a public key, which anyone can know, and a private key, which only the recipient of a message knows. These keys are mathematically linked. The message sender uses the public key to encrypt a message, and the recipient uses their private key to decrypt the message.

The word *asymmetric* is used because this method uses two different linked keys that perform inverse operations from each other whereas symmetric cryptography uses the same key to perform both operations.

It is quite straightforward to generate both the public and private key pair, but the power of asymmetric cryptography comes from the fact it is impossible for a private key to be determined from its corresponding public key. It is only the private key that needs to be kept secret in the key pair.

The primary advantage of using asymmetric encryption is that two parties don't need to pre-share a secret key to communicate using asymmetric encryption. The person encrypting a message only needs to know the recipients public key which is available to anyone on request. Then only the recipient can decrypt the message with their private key. The main disadvantage is that the asymmetric algorithm is comparatively complex when compared to symmetric encryption which means that messages take longer to encrypt and decrypt.

213

When using RSA in .NET, we used the `RSACryptoServiceProvider` class. We looked at three ways of handling our keys, using the Windows CSP to store keys, writing them out as XML (a really bad idea), and storing them in memory.

Digital Signatures

Digital signatures are based on asymmetric cryptography. For the receiver of the message, a digital signature allows the receiver to believe the correct sender sent the message; this can be thought of as a digital equivalent to a signature on a letter, except a digital signature is much harder to forge.

Digital signatures give you both authentication and non-repudiation. Authentication because the signatures have to be created by a user with a valid private key, and non-repudiation as the receiver can trust that a known sender signed the message as only, they know the private key. So, how do digital signatures do all this? Digital signatures in .NET and .NET Core are based on RSA, so some of the same rules for RSA apply for digital signatures. This is why you cannot sign data that is larger than the size of the key; that is, 1024 bits, 2048 bits, or 4096 bits. Because of this, it is common first to take a SHA-256 hash of the data that you want to sign digitally. You then use that hash to create the digital signature.

A digital signature consists of the following three algorithms:

- Public and private key generation using RSA

- A signing algorithm that uses the private key to create the signature

- A signature verification algorithm that uses the public key to test if the message is authentic

When you use RSA to encrypt data, you use the recipient's public key, and then the recipient uses their private key to decrypt the data. It is the other way around with digital signatures, to create the signature the sender uses their private key to generate the signature, and the recipient uses the sender's public key to verify the signature.

The digital signature implementation we looked at in .NET was based on RSA, so to generate the keys we use the same process as with RSA which is to use the `RSACryptoServiceProvider` class. The generation of the digital signature is handled by the `RSAPKCS1SignatureFormatter` class, and the verification of the digital signature is handled by `RSAPKCS1SignatureDeformatter`.

Hybrid Encryption

Once we had finished covering the main cryptographic primitives to cover our four pillars of cryptography (confidentiality, integrity, authentication, and non-repudiation), we then looked at combining these primitives to create a more powerful set of tools called hybrid encryption.

First, we looked at combining RSA and AES. Sharing keys securely between two or more people is very hard to do.

For asymmetric encryption, the actual process of encryption is much slower due to the modular based mathematical nature of the RSA, and there are limits to the amount of data that you can encrypt at once. A real benefit for RSA is how keys are managed. With RSA, you use a public and private key pair. The recipient of the message knows the private key, and they keep that key safe and secret; anyone can know the public key. If Alice wants to send a message to Bob, she first gets his public key. Encrypts the message with that public key and sends the message to Bob. Bob then uses his private key to read the message; which is a much better solution to keys exchange than with symmetric encryption algorithms like AES.

Now we want the best of both worlds. We want the fast and efficient encryption properties of AES coupled with the more robust key sharing mechanism of RSA. We explored hybrid encryption, which is achieved using unique symmetric session keys along with asymmetric encryption.

The sender first uses the recipient's public key to encrypt a freshly generated AES session key. The data you want to send to the recipient is encrypted with AES and that session key, and that encrypted message along with the RSA encrypted session key is sent to the recipient who then uses their private key to decrypt the session key. Once the session key is recovered, it is then used to decrypt the message.

The combination of encryption methods has various advantages. One is that a connection channel is established between two users' sets of equipment. Users can communicate using this hybrid encryption technique. A downside of asymmetric encryption is that it can slow down the encryption process, but with using it along with symmetric encryption, both of them together use their best parts, the efficiency of the symmetric encryption and the key splitting of the asymmetric encryption. The result is added security to the message sending process along with overall improved system performance.

To further extend the hybrid encryption example we added some integrity checking to the code. We wanted to add some integrity checking to ensure that the message that is sent between two people is not corrupted or tampered with in transit.

The simplest way to do this is by taking a hash of the encrypted data and the initialization vector, which could be done using any of the hashing operations, such as MD5, SHA-1, or SHA-2. The hash would be calculated after the message has been encrypted with AES and sent to the recipient inside the encrypted packet.

When the recipient wants to decrypt the message, they first recalculate the hash of the encrypted message and IV. If the hashes match, then the data is intact and hasn't been corrupted or tampered with which means the recipient can safely decrypt the message. If the hash codes do not match, then there has been an issue during transmission of the message; it has either been corrupted or tampered with, and the recipient should discard the message entirely and not trust it.

As a solution, this worked quite well, but we went one better. With the solution of hashing the encrypted data and initialization vector, nothing is stopping an attacker intercepting the message, corrupting the encrypted data or IV and then recalculating the hash. It would be much better if the strength of our session key could also protect the hashing of the data; this is possible by a hashed message authentication code or HMAC.

Like a standard hash code, a HMAC is used to verify the integrity of a message. A HMAC also allows you to verify the authentication of that message because only the person who knows the private key to recover the session key can calculate the same hash of the message. Without that session key, you cannot recalculate the same hash code of the encrypted data. A HMAC can be used with different hashing functions like MD5 or the SHA family of algorithms. In the examples in the remainder of this chapter, we use SHA-256. The cryptographic strength of an HMAC depends on the size of the key that is used.

Extending our example using HMACs for integrity provided a lot of benefits when it came to sending data from the sender to the receiver because we can detect if the encrypted messages have been corrupted or tampered with. By using a HMAC, we can ensure that the recipient can only recalculate the HMAC if they first recover the session key using their private key.

Next, we extended the example by incorporating non-repudiation with digital signatures. This means that before the sender sends the message to the recipient, the sender first takes a digital signature of the HMAC using her private key. When the recipient receives the packet of data and verifies the digital signature, if it returns true, he is confident that the original sender sent the message, and not someone else.

Combining all the cryptographic primitives this way gives you the ability to create systems that not only encrypt data but can also move that data securely between systems and detect authenticity and the potential for any tampering.

Azure Key Vault

Key management is an essential feature of any enterprise system and there are appliances like hardware security modules (HSM) that let you store keys securely. The problem with HSMs is that they are traditionally costly appliances for companies, which means they are typically used by larger organizations, such as banks or pharmaceutical companies. With the advent of cloud computing and products like Azure, we now have access to abstract HSM systems like Azure Key Vault, which brings the power of HSM to the masses.

Azure Key Vault is a service provided by Microsoft as part of their Azure cloud computing platform that makes the functionality of hardware security modules available to anyone for a fraction of the cost. Even though Microsoft is providing software abstraction to the service, underneath there is real HSM hardware. Microsoft has put into each regional data center a series of devices called nShield by Thales Security, which means that Microsoft has taken the financial hit on the cost of the hardware that they rent for a minimal price to software developers. The fundamental shift between you paying for a HSM to a pay-as-you consume module has enormous implications as this means you can now take advantage of secure key management that banks have been enjoying for many years.

Azure Key Vault lets you store encryption keys and secrets, which are encrypted blobs of text where you can safely store secret information like database connection strings or API keys to third-party systems. Azure Key Vault then lets you perform different operations as a developer such as encryption and decryption, storage and retrieval or secrets and the generation and verification of digital signatures.

When discussing Azure Key Vault, we covered five usage patterns.

- Multiple environments

- Configuration as secrets

- Local key wrapping

- Password protection

- Digital signing

Multiple Environments

The key message around environments is to make sure you do not use the same instance of Key Vault from production in your test environments. The sharing of production keys anywhere except production is a terrible idea. Instead, you should either have one additional instance of Key Vault that you use for all your test environments or script a new instance for each test environments. This does mean though, that you cannot jut copy data from production to your test environments as any data that is encrypted in production will not decrypt in your test environment, so you need to put a process in place to insert anonymized data in place of the encrypted production data.

Configuration as Secrets

Key Vault allows you to store small, named, blobs of text into Key Vault, which is very useful for storing secret data like database connection strings, API keys or anything that you wouldn't want to expose in a config file. An excellent way to think about the storage of secrets is that it is like a key-value pair NoSQL data store. You store your secret, which is the value and you give it a name which you provide when you save the value and then retrieve it again in the future.

Local Key Wrapping

When we looked at hybrid encryption, we built up an example of using RSA to encrypt an AES session key. Using Azure Key Vault, we can extend this concept by using RSA and a key stored in the vault to encrypt our local session key which means we can remove the use of `RSACryptoServiceProvider` and allow Key Vault to perform the encryption. Using this technique, you can also drastically reduce the cost of using Key Vault. You are charged per 10,000 operations on the vault. For a session, if you use Key Vault to decrypt a local AES key and then use that AES key to perform local encryption and decryption operations you are reducing the number of hops across to Key Vault which reduces your cost and also reduces latency as calling Key Vault also incurs a time penalty.

Password Protection

When we discussed password protection, I said that using a password-based key derivation function was the best current method for hashing a password where as well as providing the password to the hashing function, you also provide a salt value and a number of iterations value, so we can algorithmically slow down the hashing process.

Using a password-based key derivation function puts us in a good position, but where does Key Vault fit into this? Adding Key Vault into the equation gives a bit of extra protection. When using a Password Based Key Derivation Function (PBKDF2), we have to provide a salt and a "number of iterations" parameter, both of which need to be presented when hashing a password to compare against a stored password. Conventionally, the salt, of which you would use a new salt per password, would be stored in a database and the number of iterations might be a configuration option. The salt is not a key used for confidentiality, but why make it easy for an attacker? Using Key Vault, we can encrypt the salt before we store it in the database. Then when a user authenticates onto your system, the salt needs to be decrypted using Key Vault before the password hash is recalculated.

To successfully create a hash for a password to match a hash in your passwords table, you also need to specify the same number of iterations. If your stored password was hashed with 1000 iterations and a salt, and you try to hash the same password with the same salt but 1001 iterations, the hash will not match. This means that the number of iterations is a configuration item, which is a perfect candidate to store as a secret in Key Vault. As with salt, hiding the number of iterations isn't part of the security of a PBKDF, but why make it easy for an attacker. By storing the number of iterations as an encrypted secret in the vault, you are making their lives a little harder if they get hold of your hashed password tables as they not only have to decrypt the salt, but they have also to figure out the correct number of iterations to use, which is safely stored in the vault.

Digital Signing

The final pattern we looked at with Azure Key Vault is creating and verifying digital signatures. We looked at digital signatures back in Chapter 8 where we performed the signing and verification tasks using the RSAPKCS1SignatureFormatter and RSAPKCS1SignatoreDeFormatter classes in the .NET Framework. Signing and verification of data is a feature that Key Vault offers as part of its standard functionality, and it is straightforward to do which reduces the complexity in doing it yourself using the RSAPKCS1SignatureFormatter and deformatter classes.

Don't Forget the Perimeter

The focus of this book has been on software security with cryptography in the .NET Framework and .NET Core, but it is important to remember the perimeter of your systems. Generally, in a lot of organizations, the network and perimeter protection of your systems are handled by a specific operations team unless you are in a more DevOps-focused environment where you have access to set up perimeter security yourself. In any case, making sure any websites or web APIs that you develop sit behind HTTPS is essential. Unfortunately, a lot of people across the Internet argue that HTTPS is not required for static sites like brochureware, but this is a dangerous mindset to adopt. It is essential to make sure you always protect sites and APIs with HTTPs even if they do not specifically handle any sensitive data. Also, with many modern web browsers, warnings appear if your site is not protected with HTTPS.

Not using HTTPS means that any malicious parties cannot perform a man in the middle attack and deface the content on your site; this could be as a form of vandalism or subtly changing information on the site to unsuspecting visitors. This would typically be an attack where an attacker tries to disrupt the communication between your website and your browser.

HTTPS also protects the communications from the browser back to the server and therefore protect the privacy of your users who may be inputting sensitive information onto your site. If you are encrypting their essential data on the back end, but you do not protect the communication channel with HTTPS, then an attacker can steal their data before you get to encrypt it.

Next Steps

We have now come to the end of this book on applying cryptography with the .NET Framework and .NET Core. The next steps are for you to start implementing some of these principles in your system. I recommend that you load up and experiment with the sample code from this book which can be found on GitHub at `https://github.com/Apress/applied-crypto-.net-azure`. The best way to learn, apart from reading this book, is to take the code and experiment. Step through each of the examples in the debugger. Perhaps you could try writing some small console or terminal apps to experiment with the features. A good learning exercise is to write an application that can take any file you provide it and encrypt or decrypt it. Or perhaps using Key Vault and the hybrid encryption principles develop a small instant messaging app with peer-to-peer encryption. The techniques we have discussed in this book are very similar to the types of protocols that many instant messaging systems use today.

This book was designed to be very practical for the everyday developer. It wasn't the books intention to try and turn you into a master cryptographer but to make use of some of the tools available to you in .NET. If this book has piqued your interest, then you may want to go on and buy some of the more theoretical cryptography books. The power is in your hands now to help your employers protect their critical data for their benefit, but more importantly, their customers benefit, safety, and privacy. The power is in your hands. Use it wisely.

Thanks for reading.

Index

A

Access control lists (ACLs), 94

Advanced Encryption Standard (AES), 67
    AesManaged and
        AesCryptoServiceProvider, 73
    brute-force attacks, 69
    different key, 67
    encryption mode, 70
    initialization vector, 73
    key, 72
    padding, 72
    permutation box (P-box), 68
    rounds, 68
    substitution box (S-box), 68
    working process, 68

AesManaged and
    AesCryptoServiceProvider, 73

Ashley Madison, 3

Asymmetric encryption, 87
    key links, 87
    public key cryptography, 87

Authentication, 208

Azure Key Vault, 143, 169
    app registration, 155
    configuration, 218
    costs, 147–148
    creation, 149
    digital signing, 192
        helper class, 194
        helper method, 193

        RSAPKCS1SignatureFormatter and
          DeFormatter classes, 193
        Sha256() method, 194
        verify method, 195
    directory, 150
    hardware mode, 146
    hardware-protected key, 156
    "Hello World" application, 158
        client library, 159
        CreateKeyAsync method, 163
        DecryptAsync method, 163
        EncryptAsync method, 163
        GetAccessTokenAsync method, 160
        helper code, 162
        IKeyVault, KeyVaultBase, and
          KeyVault, 166
        IKeyVault method, 159
        keyId, 167
        KeyVault class, 161
        NuGet package, 158
        SetSecretAsync method, 164
        VaultAddress parameter, 162
        Verify method, 165

HSM hardware, 145

hybrid encryption, 195
    AesEncryption class, 198
    AES helper method, 199
    CryptographicException, 201–202
    cryptography primitives, 195
    DecryptAsync method, 201
    EncryptData method, 198–200

223

© Stephen Haunts 2019
S. Haunts, *Applied Cryptography in .NET and Azure Key Vault*,
https://doi.org/10.1007/978-1-4842-4375-6

Azure Key Vault (*cont.*)
    EncryptedPacket class, 197
    HMAC key, 200
    HMACS and digital signatures, 196
    HybridEncryption class, 202, 204
    MyKey method, 204
    private signing key, 196
    results of, 205
    Sign method, 200
    Verify method, 202
  iterations parameter, 191
  key management options, 143
  keys *vs.* secrets, 146, 153
  local key wrapping, 218
  management, 217
  multiple environments, 169, 218
    benefit of, 170
    code, configuration
      files/databases, 173
    financial data, 171
    GetSecretAsync method, 175
    KeyVault.cs class, 174
    local key wrapping (*see* Local key
      wrapping)
    production systems, 171
    separate instances, 172
    storing and retrieving
      secrets, 173
    test and production
      environments, 170
    valuable production data, 171
  nShield, 145
  password protection, 184, 218
    hashing function, 185
    helper class, 188
    key class, 189
    lines of code, 190
    PBKDF2, 186

    protect salts and iteration
      values, 187
    source code, 187–188
    steps to steps process, 190
  patterns, 169, 217
  PFX certificate file, 156
  secret code, 157
  signing and verification, 219
  software mode, 146
  software protected key, 156

B

Brute-force attacks, 69
Byte arrays, 132

C

Cipher block chaining (CBC), 71
Ciphertext feedback (CFB), 71
Ciphertext stealing (CTS), 71
Cryptographic service
    provider (CSP), 93
Cryptography
  asymmetric encryption, 213
  authentication, 208, 210
  Azure Key Vault
    configuration, 218
    key management, 217
    local key wrapping, 218
    multiple environments, 218
    password protection, 218
    patterns, 217
    signing and verification, 219
  Caesar cipher, 12
  ciphertext, 11
  data integrity, 208
  definition, 20

digital signature, 214

encryption technique, 12

enigma and mechanical
  ciphers, 15–17

hashing function, 209

history of, 208

hybrid encryption, 215

modern cryptography (*see* Modern
  cryptography)

monoalphabetic substitution
  cipher, 12

non-repudiation, 208

polyalphabetic cipher, 12

  key phrase, 14

  moveable, 13

  stationary, 13

  Vigenère cipher, 13–14

public and private key, 19

random numbers, 208

storing passwords, 210

symmetric encryption, 18, 212

D

Data breaches, 207

  consequences, 2

  cryptographic primitives, 7

  developers, 6

  financial loss, 4

  Have I Been Pwned, 2

  legal action, 4

  .NET Core 2, 10

  .NET Standard 2.0, 9

  network protection, 6

  regulatory impact, 5

  reputational damage, 5

  sensitive/confidential data, 1

  website, 1

Data Encryption Standard (DES), 61

  56-bit symmetric key, 63

  block cipher, 65

  Feistel structure, 66

  history of, 63

  internal structure, 66

  key schedule, 66

  Triple DES, 64–65

Data integrity, 113, 208

DES Challenge (DESCHALL), 18

Digital signatures, 102

  algorithms, 103

  creation, 102

  cryptography, 214

  internet websites, 102

  .NET, 106

    byte array, 109

    document modification, 111

    implementation, 109

    key generation, 106

    source code, 106

    valid options, 107

    verification, 110

  non-repudiation, 101

  process of, 103

  public and private key, 103

  verification, 105

E, F

Electronic codebook (ECB), 71

Enigma machine, 16

G

General Data Protection Regulation
  (GDPR), 5

Graphics processing units
  (GPUs), 50, 185, 211

H

Hardware security module
    (HSM), 145
Hashes, 49
Hash function
    HMAC verifies, 39
    MD5 message digest algorithm, 33–35
    message, 31
    properties of, 32
    SHA family, 35
    storing passwords
        calculation, 53
        cryptographic hashing, 49
        GenerateSalt, 51
        combine method, 51
        properties, 49
        results of, 53
        salt value, 51
        tables, 50
    unique hash code, 31
Hash message authentication codes
    (HMACs), 23, 39, 114, 210
    authentication key, 40
    dictionary attack, 41
    hash collision, 41
    hashing function, 40
    output process, 43–45
    process of, 42–43
Hybrid encryption, 113
    authentication, 114
    cryptographic primitives, 113
    cryptography, 113, 215
    digital signatures
        AssignNewKey method, 136
        benefits of, 134
        DecryptData method, 139–140
        EncryptedPacket, 136
        integrity, 138
        process, 134
        VerifySignature, 137–138
    integrity, 113, 126
        Buffer.BlockCopy operation, 130
        byte arrays, 132
        EncryptData method, 129
        EncryptedPacket class, 129
        EncryptedPacket object, 131
        HMAC, 127
        MD5, SHA-1/SHA-2, 126
        process option, 128
        session key, 130
    non-repudiation, 114
    symmetric and asymmetric (*see*
        Symmetric *vs.* asymmetric
        encryption)

I, J, K

Initialization vector (IV), 73
Integrity, 113

L

Local key wrapping
    AesCryptoServiceProvider, 177, 179
    benefits, 176
    DecryptAsync, 181
    GenerateRandomNumber
        method, 177
    key rotation and versioning, 183
    key sharing benefits, 176
    KeyVault class, 181
    master key, 182
    multiple tenants, 183
    public key, 175
    SecureRandom class, 181

M

MD5 message digest algorithm, 33–35
Modern cryptography
    authentication, 22
    blockchain, 21
    confidentiality, 22
    cryptocurrency, 21
    data integrity, 22
    non-repudiation, 23
    systems/websites, 21
Monoalphabetic substitution cipher, 12
Moore's law, 54

N

Non-repudiation, 114, 208

O

Optimal asymmetric encryption padding
        (OEAP), 96
Output feedback (OFB), 72

P, Q

Payment Card Industry–Data Security
        Standard (PCI-DSS), 5
Password Based Key Derivation Function
        (PBKDF2), 186, 211
Personally identifiable information
        (PII), 182, 207

R

Random numbers, 25
    deterministic nature, 26
    RNGCryptoServiceProvider class, 27–29
    RtlGenRandom function, 27

pseudorandom, 25
symmetric and asymmetric encryption
        keys, 27
Rivest-Shamir-Adleman (RSA), 88
    benefits, 115
    disadvantage, 88
    encryption and decryption, 90
    .NET, 91
        cryptographic service provider, 93
        encryption and decryption, 95
        in-memory keys, 91
        XML-based keys, 92
    public and private key, 88
    RSAParameters properties, 95
    XML-based keys, 98

S, T, U, V, W, X, Y, Z

Secure Hash Algorithm (SHA), 35
Side-channel timing attack, 133
Software as a service (SaaS)
        solution, 182
Storing passwords, 47
    cryptography, 210
    encryption and decryption, 48
    hashes (see Hash function)
    key derivation function, 54
        computer processors and
            GPU's, 55
        derived key, 54
        GenerateSalt, 56
        hash/encryption process, 55
        HashPassword method, 56
        Moore's law, 54
        .NET object, 55
        PBKDF2 timings, 59
        screenshot, 58
    system creation, 47–48

Symmetric *vs.* asymmetric encryption
    advantages, 116
    AesEncryption class, 123
    AES session key, 115
    DecryptData method, 121–122, 125
    decryption operation, 124
    decrypt process, 117
    Encrypt and Decrypt method, 119
    EncryptedPacket, 123
    process, 118
    results of, 126
    RSA benefits, 115
    sharing keys, 115
    short methods, 119–121
    step by step process, 116
Symmetric encryption, 18, 61
    advantage
        fast, 62
        very secure, 62
    AES (*see* Advanced Encryption
        Standard (AES))
    asymmetric encryption, 86

DES (*see* Data Encryption
        Standard (DES))
disadvantage
    compromised, 63
    symmetric key, 62
encryption and decryption, 62
.NET
    AesCryptoServiceProvider, 83
    AES encryption results, 84
    CryptoStream object, 75
    Decrypt data, 77
    DESCryptoServiceProvider, 77
    DES source code, 74
    Encrypt method, 75
    FlushFinalBlock, 76
    initialization vector, 78
    keys and initialization vectors, 74
    key variation, 82
    MemoryStream, 75
    result of, 79
    TripleDESCryptoService
        Provider, 80

CPSIA information can be obtained
at www.ICGtesting.com
Printed in the USA
LVHW101528100319
610117LV00009B/153/P

9 781484 243749